The Diary Letter

The Lost Innocence of a Young Girl

By:

Rosie Bloom

Copyright © 2015 by Rosie Bloom

All Rights Reserved.

No part of this publication may be reproduced, distributed, or transmitted in any form or by any means, including photocopying, recording, or other electronic or mechanical methods, or by any information storage and retrieval system without the prior written permission of the publisher, except in the case of very brief quotations embodied in critical reviews and certain other noncommercial uses permitted by copyright law.

Table of Contents

The Beginning of My Nightmare 7
Forever Changed 21
The Next Week 38
The Week After That 44
Making up for Lost Time 47
My First Love 52
Sharing my New Status 60
Caught in the Act 66
I'm Pregnant, Now What? 72
The Secret is Out 84
Baby Tina 89
Free to Fly 102
The Later Years 110
In the End 116
Author's Page 117
One Last Thing... 121

The Beginning of My Nightmare

I felt good for a change. Confident because I had just landed my first full-time summer job as a babysitter.

As I sat at the picnic table, watching the girls play without a care in the world, my new employer, Roy, came outside to check on us.

"How's it going?" he asked.

"Great!" I replied.

"Yeah, I think the girls will be good for you. They ain't going to give you any trouble," Roy stated.

"Yeah," I said, shaking my head in agreement.

"Hey, do you know how to drive?" he asked as he leaned across the hood of the family's bright yellow station wagon with a beer in his hand. To me, he seemed really cool and definitely intimidating.

"No," I replied swiftly and matter-of-factly.

"You wanna learn?" he asked, tipping his beer can all the way back to finish and then crushing it.

For a split second, I didn't know how to respond.

"Sure," I replied like I could mirror his swagger, even though my self-esteem was the size of a pea.

"Y'all come on, we're going for a ride," he announced, but then walked towards the house.

The girls bolted across the yard like they were running the fifty-meter dash. Everyone was barefoot but opened the car door to get in.

"Do you guys need your shoes?" I asked.

"No, we're fine barefoot," the second to the youngest replied.

As we piled into the car, Roy came out carrying a six-pack of beer. He entered the passenger seat and stuck it between his feet.

"You better do a great job driving or we'll all be walking home," he commented, although I was unsure if he was serious or joking.

I turned the ignition and the car started. Fear and excitement streamed through my body.

Roy instructed me to put my foot on the brake, pull the lever into drive, let my foot off the brake and slowly push the gas. It was so easy.

Within seconds, I was driving on the road. I felt like a million bucks. Everything was perfect. The weather was great. The girls were giddy. I was impressed with Roy's kindness. And, best of all, I was driving.

At that point, I did not think there was anything in the world that could shatter my cloud nine experience, but I couldn't have been more wrong.

Roy instructed me to take a left at the next road. I put my blinker on and proceeded to turn. As I did, I noticed Roy had slid across the seat toward me. Initially, I thought I turned to hard. Just as fast, I knew that my driving wasn't the problem.

"Do you have any hair on your pussy?" he whispered in my ear.

Time stood still as the impact of his question sent a severe shockwave through my body. My heart was beating so fast I thought I was having a heart attack and a band of sweat formed across my forehead.

"Does that make you hot?" Roy questioned as he slid back into the passenger seat. He was confident about his ability to make me nervous with a smirk on his face that baffled me to no end. Out of the corner of my eye, I could see his jaw moving, like he was gritting his teeth back and forth, waiting for an answer.

I said nothing.

I was fifteen and panic-stricken over his question.

I had zero experience with boys other than being picked on at school because of my academic struggles, looks, and stature. My overweight five-foot-ten-inch frame attracted a lot of unwanted attention. My long, stringy brown hair and coke bottle glasses did not help my situation, nor did being pulled out of regular classes to attend with the "special" group of students.

I was a hopelessly awkward teenager who had one goal in mind: to make some money for the summer.

That's where Roy came into play.

I had just met Roy a couple days earlier while I was babysitting for his neighbors, Mack and Lynn, although I use the term neighbor loosely because their houses were at least half a mile apart.

I had their two babies, aged seven months and two years, outside, letting them play when Roy stopped at the end of the driveway.

"Hey," he yelled out.

I figured he was someone Mack and Lynn knew because the road was very secluded.

"Hi," I said, picking up the seven-month-old and putting her on my hip as I walked closer to the road.

"I'm looking for a babysitter for the summer. You know anybody that'd be interested?"

"I would," I told him.

Roy asked me about my babysitting abilities and I told him I loved children and had taken care of many, although, in reality, I had only cared for Mack and Lynn's children a handful of times and my little sister when my mom needed to go somewhere.

Roy told me about his family. He had five girls aged 5, 7, 8, 9, and 11. He and his wife, Dawn, both worked and were interested in finding care for their girls for the summer.

School was about to let out in a week, so I desperately wanted the job. The thought of having full-time work with full-time pay was appealing. Plus, I wouldn't be stuck at home bored all day.

Roy wrote his number on a piece of paper and told me to call Dawn to arrange a meeting.

As soon as I got home from babysitting that day, I called the house and Dawn answered the phone. She sounded so sweet and was eager to have someone to watch over their girls. She explained my basic duties as a provider, which seemed simple enough: make lunch and ensure nobody got hurt.

We arranged to meet on Saturday, which was only two days away. My mom drove me to their residence, as I did not have a driver's license.

As we pulled into the driveway, the five girls that were outside playing ran up to our old beat up car and surrounded it.

I wasn't put off by their little dilapidated house with junk spread all over the yard because we lived in similar conditions. The barely standing barn sat off to the side with barbed wire fencing to keep the animals contained. They had horses and pigs, from what I could see, as well as cats and dogs.

It truly looked like an animal farm.

Their run-down house was secluded in the countryside with nothing but wide open fields, which was then lined with woods surrounding them. Poverty was high in our area, so I was used to the living conditions of the underprivileged.

Upon getting out of the car, my mom immediately recognized Dawn from Bingo. My mom's demeanor changed when they "officially" met. It was as if a burst of energy hit her instantly. It was encouraging to see her brighten up.

My mom had struggled with depression for as long as I could remember, and she was a loner. She played Bingo on occasion, but not often because we were so poor. She never worked outside the home, but I often wondered if that would have helped her. My mom was sad about everything: the way she looked (my mom was a much shorter and wider version of me), her financial situation (we never had money and had always been on government assistance), her marriage to my dad (they were more like roommates than a couple), her childhood (apparently she felt unloved and unwanted all of her life) and even the television shows she watched. So seeing her come alive around Dawn made me happy.

As they continued chatting about the different Bingo venues they went to, Roy came outside. He introduced himself and then instructed the girls to line up for a formal introduction. Roy may have been a small guy, with his five feet six inches frame, but his voice was commanding and firm. He had a distinctive olive colored skin tone that stemmed from an Indian bloodline. His physique was great and he had jet black hair that kind of reminded me of Elvis Presley. Even though Roy was in his late twenties, he didn't look much older than a teenager.

In a military like fashion, the girls lined up in order. Each daughter was ordered to speak when called upon. His antics were quite unusual to me. Regardless, I could tell each girl's personality was distinct.

Amy, the oldest of the five, with her dirty blonde hair and bluntly cut bangs was like a mom to her younger siblings. For eleven, she acted very mature and seemed helpful in so many ways.

Tara, the second child, was chubby with a round full face and darker hair like her dad. She was whiney. Everything that didn't benefit her caused a problem and she was very vocal in letting everyone know how she felt.

Rachel, the middle child, was skinny and awkward with thin, flat brown hair. It was evident that she had a learning disability, one that I identified with myself. Rachel was quiet and withdrawn. When she did speak, her speech impediment was obvious.

Mary was the life of the party. She had more energy than everyone put together. She did not demand anyone's attention, but her joyful personality made you want to be around her. Although Mary was dressed like a tomboy, her beauty was unmistakable with her big brown eyes and soft brown hair.

Penny was the baby of the family. She stood out with her birthmark in the middle of her forehead. I don't know if she could have been classified as a spoiled brat because there wasn't much to be spoiled with, but Penny got what she wanted when she wanted it.

After the introduction, Roy ordered the girls to go play. As much as they wanted to be around the adults, by the look on Roy's face, it was obvious that wasn't an option.

I followed the girls around a little bit so I could interact with them. They seemed so happy to have me there. I felt the same way.

I eventually made my way back over to my mom, Dawn, and Roy. I was shocked at how chatty my mom was, as I had never heard her talk that much.

Roy finally chimed in and recommended that my mom and Dawn go out that evening so he could watch me interact with his girls. My sister, Eva, who was 9, stayed with us as well.

My mom and Dawn objected slightly to the idea of going out, but Roy was insistent that they go. Actually, he demanded it. Dawn obeyed his order and grabbed her purse. They decided to catch the early session of Bingo on a nearby Indian reservation.

As we watched them pull off, all I could think about was how great life was at that moment. I had a babysitting job, my mom had a new friend, and my sister had the opportunity to play with other girls.

I was so thankful.

Roy had disappeared into the house for a little while, but then came back out shortly thereafter. I don't think my mom and Dawn had been gone for more than thirty minutes when he offered to teach me how to drive.

I was doing great behind the wheel and everything about that evening was priceless—until he asked me *that question*.

I had never been so embarrassed in all my life. My reaction was out of pure fright over his boldness for asking me about my private area. Every thought imaginable passed through my brain. No response seemed appropriate so I shut down.

I focused on the road and drove to the best of my new ability, but I did not say a word. Out of the corner of my eye, I could see Roy staring at me, his eyes piercing through every inch of my body. Silence seized the front seat, and my white knuckles glowed as I clutched the wheel. Roy was carefully watching my body language.

A squeal from the back seat broke his gaze. Roy's daughters and my little sister were having the time of their life while I felt mine hang in the balance.

Roy finally suggested that we should probably head back to his house. I agreed, and once I spoke, Roy immediately started talking like nothing had happened moments earlier. The only thing I had hoped for was that he didn't make any more comments about my private parts. That made me super uncomfortable.

Twenty minutes later we arrived safely back at Roy and Dawn's and all of us poured out of the car. As soon as we walked into the house, Roy asked me to get him a beer.

My God, this guy can drink a lot! I thought as I went to the refrigerator.

More than anything, I just wanted to go home. His question made me really nervous, but I played it off like it wasn't bothering me.

The girls and I sat around the kitchen table talking and playing, waiting for my mom and Dawn to come back from Bingo. Roy chimed in occasionally, but he pretty much focused on the television program that was on while he continuously drank beer.

Not soon enough for me, we heard a car pull into the driveway. They were home. I breathed a sigh of relief, knowing I was just moments away from leaving.

My mom and Dawn came in the house, happily announcing that my mom had won two-hundred fifty dollars. We were all ecstatic! My thoughts finally relented on Roy's question and started to focus on what my mom could buy me with all that money. That, of course, was a lot of money to us.

In the midst of the commotion, my mom claimed she felt lucky and wanted to take her chances again tomorrow. Dawn completely agreed and looked at Roy for permission. Roy was pretty intoxicated by this time but told them they could go if I would stay and watch the girls. All eyes fixed on me. How did I just become the center of attention?

I did not want to break my mom's heart; she seemed so happy. It was like Roy and Dawn gave her a joy that had been long-missed.

"Yeah, I can watch the girls tomorrow," slipped out of my mouth.

In my heart, I was crushed, but the smile on my mom's face felt worth it.

Once I agreed, Roy suggested I sleep over. My heart sank, but I felt somewhat secure knowing that Dawn and the five girls were in the house. My mom said she was okay with me sleeping over and that she would bring me a bag of clothes and toiletries in the morning. She told my little sister Eva it was time to go, and they left. (Eva was too scared to sleep anywhere so that is why she didn't stay.)

Right after they had gone, we all went to bed. I slept with Roy and Dawn's two oldest girls, Amy and Tara. The other three girls—Rachel, Mary, and Penny—slept in the room next door. There were four bedrooms upstairs; each had a full-size bed and a dresser but no closet. The hallway was a total of seven feet long, if that. All the walls were covered in dark paneling and the carpet on the floor was pieced together with duct tape. All I could think was, "and I thought we were poor," and we were, but seeing their living conditions made me appreciate mine a little more.

The next morning, all I could smell was bacon cooking. I was so hungry since we didn't eat dinner the night before. We all got up and made our way downstairs where Dawn had a prepared a full spread of breakfast food.

Dawn seemed like a nice lady. She was heavy-set like me, although much shorter. She kept her straight light brown hair pulled back in a ponytail and used a curling iron to curl her bangs under. Her blue eyes and soft tone seemed like an awkward match to Roy. I had heard a few times that opposites attract… and there it was in front of me.

The mood at the kitchen table was one of excitement, as the girls were happy that I slept over and there was a lot of food to eat. I filled my plate with eggs, bacon, toast, and pancakes and scarfed breakfast down like I hadn't eaten in days.

"You better slow down piggy," Roy said to me.

Instantly I felt sick to my stomach. That comment stung like an entire wasps nest attacking me.

Roy then made a remark that I could help the pigs when he got ready to feed them. Dawn stuck up for me and told Roy to shut up. He shot her a look that scared me and walked outside.

The searing pain of his statement was not letting up, even after he left. I broke on the inside but did not shed a tear, at least not at their house.

After all of us ate, I helped Dawn wash and put away the dishes. She didn't say a word, which made it kind of awkward for me. Once we finished in the kitchen, she decided to get ready for Bingo. The girls and I decided to go outside and play. Everything about these girls screamed that they were dying for attention. They loved that I was there, but it was somewhat overwhelming because all five of them wanted me to watch them do something—all at the same time. Outside was their safe haven, and the clean refreshing air made it even better. There was plenty of room to play, unlike the tiny space inside the house.

Right before lunch, my mom showed up to get Dawn. The first thing she announced was that she was sorry she forgot my bag. I didn't care; I was so happy to see her. I asked her where Eva was, to which she said she stayed home with my dad to help him do some work in the field. I believed it. Eva loved our dad.

He was a man of few words who, I think, internalized everything.

Although I had inherited my height from him, he was unlike me in that he was very withdrawn from everything and everyone. At our house, we called him the gentle giant, but we probably should have called him the silent giant. He was so disconnected from life, never making a decisive choice about anything. Honestly, he was just an adult body in the house. My mom and dad hardly ever talked, although we ate dinner together often. It was clear my parents were not happy, but they continued to coexist under the same roof.

As my mom pulled up, Dawn, now in better spirits, emerged from the house and Roy came out of the barn. I had wondered where he went, but I dared not ask after the small tiff at breakfast. Roy greeted my mom and told Dawn to go win some money. He then made his way into the house.

As my mom and Dawn got into the car, all of us wished them luck and told them to bring home the jackpot so we could be rich.

As they pulled away, the girls said they were a little hungry. I told them I'd make them something to eat and followed them into the house.

Roy was sitting in his normal spot at the kitchen table, his ashtray overflowing with cigarette butts.

"Becky, grab me a beer, would ya?" he asked as soon as we walked through the door.

As I walked by him, because the refrigerator was literally one foot from where he sat, his hand brushed my ass. I was stunned. *Maybe it was an accident*, I tried to reason. After all, his children were *right there* in the kitchen with us.

I handed him his beer and he thanked me with a grin on his face. It dawned on me that it was no accident. At this point, I didn't know how to act. The security I had felt the night before instantly dissipated; these girls were not a safety net. Coming to terms with that was completely unnerving.

"Hey, why don't you give the girls some lunch so they can all take a nap?" he told me.

"Sure, no problem. That's what we came in the house for anyways," I told him, wondering why they have to take a nap on the weekend. I dared not question his authority.

I looked through the cabinets and found the peanut butter and bread. I took out six paper plates and placed two slices of bread on each. I was a little hesitant to eat, but I too was hungry. I was hopeful he'd keep all his comments to himself.

"I want jelly on mine." Mary said.

"Me too!" Rachel chimed in.

"Okay, who wants jelly?" I asked to get an accurate headcount. Four hands went up. I headed towards the fridge to grab the jelly and got the surprise of a lifetime from Roy as I felt him forcefully grab my ass. This was by no means an accident. When I turned to look at him, all he said was, "Grab me another beer, will ya?" I was stunned.

I grabbed him a beer, placing it in front of him, trying to watch his hands. I reached back into the refrigerator for the jelly and finished making the sandwiches. I could feel Roy's stare the entire time I prepared lunch. I passed the sandwiches out to each girl and we ate.

I prayed Roy wouldn't say anything about me eating, which he did not.

As soon as we finished, we all threw our paper plates in the trash can. As I was putting the ingredients away, Roy told the girls to go upstairs for a nap.

Rachel whined that she wasn't tired and Roy lit up like some firecrackers. In one second flat, he was across the room in Rachel's face asking her what she just said. Rachel said nothing, shaking her head *no*, choking back her tears. His rage was real and the confrontation was terrifying. As soon as he stepped back, Rachel ran through the living room and up the stairs. The other four sisters immediately followed her. Because I was scared, I started to go with them.

That's when everything changed.

Forever Changed

"Hey, where are you going?" Roy said sternly.

"I was going to go lay down with them," I replied, unsure of my role as a babysitter with their dad in the house.

"No, you're not going up there. They're fine. Come sit down," he told me.

I took a seat in a chair on the opposite side of the kitchen table.

"No, here," he said, pointing at the seat right next to him.

I got up and sat down in the chair next to him. Panic had set in and my forehead beaded with sweat once again.

"You never answered my question last night," he said, with a smirk on his face, and completely ignoring my perspiration.

I couldn't talk. I didn't know what to say. How was I to respond to such a question?

"Talk to me," he waited with anticipation and like he was a concerned friend.

"Yea, I do," I finally replied. My stomach was in knots. I had never talked to anyone about any body part ever. Besides, I wasn't particularly fond of anything about myself. The entire situation felt wrong on so many levels.

He leaned all the way back in his chair to finish his beer. As he set the empty can on the table, he asked me to get him another one.

I got up and, when I opened the fridge, he swung around in his seat and stood up behind me. He grabbed me from behind and put one hand on my breast and one hand between my legs and pressed his body into mine. I could feel his erection through his pants.

"I want to see the hair on your pussy," he whispered in my ear.

Even though the refrigerator door was open, my whole body broke out in a sweat. Fear paralyzed me. He said it again, and I was finally able to muster up enough strength to shake my head no.

"Come on," he begged, turning me around as he unzipped his pants. His penis was fully erect as he rubbed it on me. I was shocked. I had never seen one before. His hands moved quickly and before I knew it my pants were undone and his fingers were near my privates.

I finally spoke. "No, Roy, stop."

He shushed me and told me to be quiet because the girls were sleeping.

"I don't want to do this," I pleaded with him.

"It's okay, just be quiet," he urged.

At that moment, he let go of me. He adjusted his penis to put it back in his pants.

"Why don't you go check on the girls?" he said.

At that point, going anywhere but near him was okay with me. I walked around the kitchen table, through the living room and up the only set of stairs in this tiny house. I took a deep breath as I made it to the top, partly because I was so out of shape and partly because I wanted to think about my options in the seconds that I had.

I opened the door to the first bedroom and found Rachel and Penny asleep. Mary was just laying in the bed, playing with her fingers. She closed her eyes when I looked at her, but I'm sure that was because she did not want to get in trouble. As I took three steps to the next bedroom over, I heard footsteps coming up the stairs. My heart pounded like a hammer driving a nail.

I popped the door open to the second bedroom, where Amy and Tara were whispering to each other. They looked at me like they were scared and closed their eyes. It was a set up; I was trapped and had no way out.

As soon as I shut the door, Roy was standing behind me. He had his finger pressed to his mouth for me to be quiet. He used his body to block the entire hallway as he nudged me into his and Dawn's bedroom. I stood there quietly as he closed the door. I couldn't help but notice the bulge in his pants as I looked around. It was evident that he was still aroused.

He quickly and quietly slipped his pants and underwear off and stepped to me, fully erect.

"You have to be quiet," he said softly as he unbuttoned my pants and started pushing them down. I felt frozen in time, like there was no way this could actually be happening.

"The girls aren't sleeping," I whispered while shaking my head no. I was so scared and my heart was beating so fast I thought it was going to explode in my chest. Do I scream, run, punch him in the face? Everything inside told me this wasn't right, but I honestly didn't know what to do. I had never experienced anything even remotely close to what was happening in that moment. My body felt like it was shutting down with fear; numbness engulfed me.

Roy grabbed my arms and guided me over to the bed until I fell back. He got on top of me, but my feet were still in my pants so he couldn't spread my legs. He got up quickly and took my pants and underwear off one foot and crawled back on top of me. As he mounted me, my mind blanked out. I wanted to pass out, but I felt his hand push my inner thigh outward so he could put his penis in. The penetration as he pushed himself into me made me gasp in pain. I cried out that it hurt and to stop. He took a few more pumps and told me to hold on. It was over in a matter of seconds, but the pain was excruciating.

Then he got up like nothing ever happened. He put his underwear and pants back on and told me to get up. Terrified, I swiftly got off the bed and slipped my clothes back on. He opened the bedroom door and motioned for me to go. I did, and he followed me down the stairs. I immediately went to the bathroom, as I felt wetness that I had never experienced before.

As I pulled my pants down, blood and goo soaked my panties. When I wiped down there, it not only hurt, but the tissue was full of blood and semen. I was at a loss and had no idea what I should do. I could only wish my mom had brought me a change of clothes, but she had forgotten them.

I grabbed some tissue to clean up as much of the mess that I could. I remember sitting on the toilet staring at my blood-soaked underwear for what seemed like thirty minutes. I snapped out of my traumatized state when I heard the girls.

"Can we get up?" Tara called out to her dad.

"Yea, y'all get up," he replied back to them.

It sounded like a stampede of elephants coming down the stairs. I tried to hurry out of the bathroom. When I emerged, Roy was sitting at the table with a pistol in front of him. The events of what had just happened had me in a state of shock.

The girls watched me like a hawk watching its prey, knowing something was terribly wrong but dared not say a word. This was truly the quietest the girls had ever been, as they kept a close distance among themselves.

Roy asked if I wanted to go outside to shoot his gun. He acted so normal, as though nothing had happened. He was actually in a good mood, or so it appeared.

Deep down inside, I just wanted to leave, but I mustered out a yes, that I would go outside. I grabbed the girls some chips, juice, and cups and headed for the door.

Roy told Mary to grab him a beer out of the fridge, which she did. I set everything down on the picnic table and started getting the snacks ready for the girls. Each one sat down and was still eerily quiet.

Roy loaded the gun and pointed it into the open field with a wooded backdrop. It seemed like the perfect place for anyone to shoot a gun. They lived in an extremely remote area.

"Have you ever shot one of these before?" Roy asked me as he waved his pistol in the air.

"No," my reply was short.

"Here, give it a shot," he said, putting the gun in my hand. I wish putting a bullet to the head of the man who just attacked me would have crossed my mind, but it didn't, nor would I have even considered it with his five girls watching. Everything I did that day was just going through the motions. There was no thought or feeling behind my simple actions. I was a far cry from the normal girl I was just the day before.

I extended my arm completely straight and aimed the gun into the wide open field and empty woods. When I pulled the trigger, the bang from the gun startled me. It was like it woke me up from the out-of-body experience that I felt like I was having. I looked at Roy and told him I was done, and that shooting a gun was not really my cup of tea.

"Looks like your prints are all over the gun," he said with a smirk on his face, almost laughing about it. What was he talking about? I didn't fully comprehend the meaning of his statement. He stepped closer to me and softly said, "I'd hate to see you or your family killed if any false information got out."

My heart immediately sank to my feet. I knew then his threat was as real as the rape that happened just a few minutes ago. It felt like a bomb had just exploded on my insides. All these emotions were brand new to me, and I was having a hard time keeping it all together.

Just then, my mom and Dawn pulled in from Bingo. All the girls ran to the car.

As Roy and I strolled slowly to the car, he started talking quietly, "I'm telling you right now if you tell anyone, I'll kill your family and make it look like you did it. Your fingerprints are all over the gun. And if you decide not to come to work tomorrow or any day I come to pick you up, I'm going to assume you told someone and I'll have to take care of it. You understand me?"

I nodded my head, still fixated on making it to my mom's car. By this time, the girls had been informed that their mom didn't win any money. Even though they didn't win any money, it seemed like my mom and Dawn had a nice day out. It was far from the tragic event that took place just a little while ago.

"Mom, I don't feel so well. Can we go home?" I asked. I could feel Roy's eyes on me as my eyes pleaded with fear. My mom completely missed my signal.

Roy quickly interjected, "Naw, just stay a while. Mary, go get three beers."

Dawn immediately said she didn't want one, but my mom said she'd have one and that was it. I was crushed. Did she not hear me? It felt like it took my mom three hours to drink one beer, but she said she'd have one, and that was all she had.

During that one beer, she asked a lot of questions about my babysitting performance. Roy answered everything like I was the queen of England. He praised every detail he could think of and made me sound beyond great. Dawn asked the girls a few questions and was completely happy with the responses. She definitely loved the fact that they liked me. The girls didn't say a word about their dad coming upstairs; it seemed as though everything that happened earlier was a distant memory now that my mom and Dawn were back. That is, a distant memory to everyone but me.

We left to go home right after my mom was done, even though Roy was insistent that we stay. Obviously, he was a hard man to refuse. As soon as we got home, my mom questioned me about how I liked babysitting for Roy and Dawn. She wanted to know if I felt like I could handle all five girls. I told her the girls weren't a problem at all, but left off what Roy had done to me. Perhaps because my demeanor was consistently quiet and I didn't have an outgoing personality, she completely missed the signs that something was seriously wrong.

After our short conversation, I immediately went into the bathroom to shower. I wanted to wash away the horrific events of the afternoon. I felt so different, having been assaulted, that it was like I was washing someone else's body.

Once I was finished, I went to my room for the rest of the evening and replayed the rape in my mind for hours. I tried to analyze everything that happened between me and Roy. I pondered over telling someone what had happened, but nothing about revealing this situation seemed right. I really felt that I played a part in what happened, even though I did nothing to warrant that kind of abuse.

The future seemed so bleak to me. If I told and he killed my family, would I go to jail for life for a crime I didn't commit? Would Roy go to jail, forcing Dawn to raise the girls alone? Would Dawn blame and be mad at me for what happened? Would Roy hate me forever? Maybe it was an isolated incident and would never happen again? I didn't know, and it seemed impossible to quiet my mind as it raced a thousand miles a minute.

I moped around on Sunday, not really sure of what I should do. My mom, dad, and sister seemed oblivious to my extremely somber mannerisms. I did not want to come out and tell anyone, but I was hoping someone would ask me what was wrong and then dig deep so I could release all the pent up anxiety about the rape. That didn't happen.

Everyone carried on at my house like everything was completely normal, even though it was so far from it. I was dying inside.

The phone rang and broke my racing thoughts. It was Dawn, calling to ensure that I would be available for babysitting first thing in the morning. My mom took the call and told her how much I enjoyed their girls. As they chatted, I overheard my mom comment on the difficulty of Dawn's job. I heard my mom gasp several times and claim that there was no way she could perform the duties required of Dawn. I walked into the kitchen so I could hear some more about Dawn's job. My mom let me listen in as Dawn explained some of her responsibilities.

Dawn worked in a group home with severely mentally retarded and disabled adults. The position required a GED, which Dawn ultimately received so she could work for the state. The demands of her employment often involved grueling and unfathomable tasks. Dawn told my mom that she had been kicked, bitten, pinched and punched by the clients that lived in the home. She had also been smeared with feces and urinated on many times. I felt bad that Dawn had to work so hard under terrible conditions. I had no idea jobs like that even existed and immediately knew it was not something I would be interested in.

When they hung up, my mom reiterated to me that Roy would pick me up at about 7:30 a.m. I had heard Dawn say it, and, although my body ached as she talked, I knew I had to be ready. I had to go back because Dawn needed to work.

I had no idea my life would change so dramatically at the hands of one married man.

Please, Not Again…

The next morning, Roy arrived right on time. I could feel his cold eyes on me as I closed the front door to my house and walked to his van with my head down. As much as my mind was screaming *no*, I opened the passenger door and climbed in.

"Good morning, beautiful," he said, as though that was supposed to make me feel better.

"Hey," was all that came out of my mouth as I blankly stared ahead.

"What's wrong with you? You start your period or something?" he said sarcastically, with that same old smirk on his face.

I couldn't even respond. Was this asshole serious? Did he really not know what was wrong with me? Although he scared the shit out of me, I didn't want to be overly nice to him and make him think I wanted to have sex again. I wanted to do my job and that was it, nothing more.

"How was the rest of your weekend?" he asked.

My answers were short on purpose because I didn't know how to respond. I was petrified of Roy, unsure of how to handle our conversation. "Fine," I replied, keeping my emotions buried deep inside.

"You go out with your mom shopping?" he questioned.

Why was he being so nice? Was I supposed to act like nothing happened between us? Was this his way of saying he was sorry and wouldn't rape me again? Or was this his way of saying he wanted me for a second time? His passive aggressive behavior confused me. I felt tormented by my reality.

"No, we just stayed at home," I told him.

Within six minutes, we arrived at the house and both of us got out. As we walked inside, Dawn had the girls' breakfast ready. She immediately gave me instructions on what they would eat for lunch and after nap snacks. She told the girls to be good for me and kissed Roy on the lips.

She looked him in the eyes and said, "I love you," before she walked out the door to leave for work.

He replied, "I love you, too. Have a good day."

The connection between them didn't feel or look genuine. I could not pinpoint what was off, but I had not seen them interact in this manner before. It was awkward.

Roy was only minutes behind her, as he said he had a full day ahead of him. He was a traveling salesman that sold baked goods from his van. As he headed out the door, he said he'd see me later, but it didn't register to me that he would actually *see me later*.

The girls and I cleaned up the morning breakfast mess and headed outside. We had to take advantage of all the nice weather we had been having.

As lunch time rolled around, I went inside to prepare their food. I called them in after I had each plate set on the table. They were extremely hungry, as they had run around outside playing all morning. All of them ate like they had missed their morning meal, even though they had not.

After lunch, Dawn had given me specific instructions that they were to take a nap. It would give me a chance to clean up and take a break from the busyness of five girls.

Just as they were finishing up, I heard a vehicle pull into the driveway. I felt sick to my stomach, like I had just been punched. I peeked out the window and my knees went weak. It was Roy. What was he doing home? My mouth went completely dry.

He walked into the house and ordered the girls to 'get their asses upstairs' for their nap.

'What's the rush?' I thought. As they hurried to use the bathroom before their nap, he told me to make him some lunch. I put together two ham sandwiches and placed them on the table where he normally sat. The girls ran up the stairs like they had just seen a ghost and were really scared. Surely, this wasn't about to happen again?

He sat down and ate his lunch quickly. I tried to not watch him wolf his food down, but I was super anxious, almost anticipating what was to come.

As soon as he got done eating, he told me to get him some juice, like I was his live-in maid. I immediately got it for him, hoping he would drink it and then go back to work. I sat back down in the chair at the other end of the table. I didn't want to be near him, but I swear he could hear my heart beat in my chest from across the kitchen.

"Kids been giving you a hard time?" he asked.

"No, they've been good all morning," I responded with my heart still beating fast and my mouth feeling like I had just swallowed one hundred cotton balls.

"Well, here, let me give you a hard time," he said as he got up from the table and walked towards me. The smirk on his face said he was playing, but his actions said differently.

I shook my head no, but it didn't matter. He had pulled his penis out of his pants and started rubbing it on my arm and t-shirt.

"Here, suck on it for a minute," he demanded as he shoved my head into his penis. At first I kept my lips closed, but the tightness he had on my long brown hair made me open up. I was gagging, which infuriated him.

"You don't know how to suck cock?" he asked me, but I couldn't answer.

"Ah forget it," he said, pulling me up out of the chair by my hair. He let go of my hair just long enough to unbutton my shorts. Why did it feel like he had eight hands when I only saw two? I said 'no' softly, but he pretended he didn't hear me. I said it again a little louder and he told me to shut up as he pulled me into the living room where the sofa was.

"Lay down," he whispered, looking straight into my eyes.

I did what I was ordered, shaking my head *no* the entire time. He pulled my shorts all the way down and threw them to the side of the couch. He got on top of me and pushed his penis into me with all of his strength. The pain was so intense that I yelped.

"Shut up, shut up, shut up," he said. "Just shut up, I'm almost done." Thirty seconds later, he got up off of me and pulled his pants up—zipped, buckled and belted in two seconds flat. I laid on the couch, unable to move. I couldn't believe this just happened again. It hurt so badly.

He bent over to grab my shorts and underwear and threw them on top of me.

"Get up," he stated firmly.

I ran to the bathroom naked from the waist down. I sat on the toilet, where a mixture of his semen mixed with my blood oozed out of my vagina. I did my best to wipe gently, but I really wanted this mess to disappear. I slipped my underwear and shorts back on and exited the bathroom. He was standing at the kitchen door about to leave.

"I'll see you later, okay? I got to go back to work," he said and walked out the door. I stared at him blankly. My only thought was, *what do you mean 'I'll see you later, okay?' Is this going to happen again?*

He started his vehicle and when I heard it pull away, I broke down crying. Why is this happening? What is wrong with him? What is wrong with me? My whole body was shaking with fear. I couldn't process anything in my brain. Everything about this situation was wrong. I couldn't fathom continuing to work for him, but at the time, I feared for my life—and my family's lives. I feared Dawn's reaction. I feared my mom's distress and heartbreak. I was at a loss.

After Roy raped me and left, I went upstairs to check on the girls. Amy and Tara were awake, and there is no doubt in my mind that they heard everything that had just transpired. When I opened the door, Amy asked me if I was okay. I shook my head *yes*, but even this eleven-year-old could tell that I wasn't. I told the girls they could get up. Mary heard us and got out of the bed as well.

It had just started raining, so, unfortunately, we would not be going outside. I turned on the television and let the girls' watch it until Dawn got home. Dawn questioned them, as well as me, as to how the girls behaved. She wanted to make sure they did not act up on my watch. Dawn also asked me if I was comfortable taking care of them without Roy there. I told her everything was fine and the girls were great.

Dawn was clueless about what was going on. Nobody said Roy had come home for lunch and she didn't suspect a thing. All five daughters were terrified of him; it was evident from the way they acted around him, and I couldn't blame them. Heck, I was terrified of him. Roy had a presence about him that you didn't dare cross.

Dawn offered to run me home, which I happily accepted. When she dropped me off, she let me know that Roy would be at my house in the morning to pick me up to babysit again tomorrow. I told her okay, like everything was normal, even though it was far from normal. I walked into the house consumed with guilt and overwhelmed with such a heaviness that it felt like I had an elephant sitting on my chest.

I immediately showered when I got inside my house. As the water flowed out of the shower and onto my face, I couldn't help but wonder if the kids would spill the beans. I pictured Tara and Amy telling their mom what happened earlier in the day and I saw Dawn's pain and anger in my mind's eye. The burden of playing out that movie in my head was too much. From there, I became consumed with Roy's threat of killing my family and sending me to jail. I tried holding back my sobs in the shower as I imagined trying to explain to court officials that it wasn't me, that I had been set up. My insides felt achy with fear—if that's even possible.

I ended my shower, hoping to stop my overactive mind. I retreated to my room for the rest of the evening, but I had no control over the thoughts that ravished my brain. I didn't want to think about my situation, yet I had no control over my thoughts. My biggest wish for that evening was that the girls not tell their mom what Roy was doing to me. I definitely didn't want her to be mad at me.

How I fell asleep eluded me, but I did not wake up until the next morning.

The Next Week

Roy picked me up for work every morning, Monday through Friday. Over that week, he did not come home at lunch time to rape me. I was relieved not to see him but wondered if something was going on. Did Dawn suspect something? Maybe the girls accidentally slipped up and said something. I tried to watch everyone to see if anything was going on, but there was nothing I could detect. Regardless, I survived the week with little anxiety.

When Dawn arrived home that Friday afternoon, she put my weekly salary in cash in my hands and then asked me: "Would you like to babysit tomorrow for a few hours so your mom and I can go to Bingo?"

Everything inside of me screamed *no*, but a *yes* flew out of my mouth.

How could I say *no* to an adult?

Plus, I liked Dawn. She took care of the girls, catered to Roy's every demand and worked. To me, she was like Superwoman, and I admired her tenacity that held it all together.

Dawn brought me home that Friday night, but just long enough to grab my clothes so I could spend the night. It was Roy that recommended that I stay overnight. Dawn and the girls were excited by the idea, and I did not want to make it seem that there was anything wrong. Roy sure did know how to manipulate a situation so that it would benefit him.

When we got back to Dawn and Roy's house, it became perfectly clear that Roy had been drinking. Apparently, he had stopped by the local bar and had some shots of liquor with a few guys. Even though he stumbled around the house, he continued to drink. It was the first time I had ever seen Roy that drunk.

Within minutes of our arrival, his behavior became obscene. He began to flirt with me in front of Dawn, which made me extremely uncomfortable. He joked about how it would take a ladder to mount me (sexually), how he was going to spend all my money on beer (because I had just gotten paid), even how big my ass was (although to look at me and Dawn, we had the same build, though I was seven inches taller than she was).

Dawn laughed at his jokes and comments, but I could tell she was not happy with him. On occasion, she told him to stop talking like that and to knock it off, but he replied back with a "who you think you're talking to like that?" with an underlying tone of 'I will kick your ass if you don't shut up.'

I tried to distance myself from the situation by hanging out in the living room with the girls, but that only made Roy get louder with his comments. Dawn finally convinced him to go to bed, and we watched him stumble up the stairs. I felt a little more relaxed, knowing that he was too drunk to try anything with me.

As the girls got sleepy, I opted to go to bed with them. I slept with Amy, who was the oldest. We talked for a little while about what we wanted to be when we grew up. I told her I wanted to be a veterinarian because I loved animals. She confessed that she wanted to help young girls get away from mean men. That comment solidified that not only did she know what her dad was doing to me, but she felt compassion towards my situation. I felt like I bonded with Amy that night.

The next morning came and Dawn was taking care of all her motherly and wifely duties: breakfast, laundry, dishes and picking up the messes scattered throughout the house. After she was done, she announced that she was going to get ready. Roy went outside to the barn, and the girls and I watched some television. Shortly thereafter, my mom showed up to get Dawn for their day out. Unfortunately, the weather was bad and we were stuck inside.

Eventually, Roy made it back inside the house. He went to the fridge and grabbed a beer, even though it was only about eleven a.m. After drinking about four of them, Roy decided to go downstairs to the cellar, apparently to tinker with something. The cellar was dark, dingy, and musty. It had a dirt floor that—I'm assuming—gave off the odor, and the walls were made of rough concrete. Roy was only down there for about five minutes before we heard him bark his orders.

"Becky, come hold this pipe," he yelled up the stairs. Amy looked at me and must have seen the fear in my eyes.

"I can hold it, Dad," Amy answered before I could say anything.

"You're not strong enough," he said like he was angry that she replied. "Becky, get your ass down here right now and hold this pipe."

As I took my first step, he peeked up at me and softly said, "Close the door." I shut the door behind me. I knew what was about to happen. As I got to the bottom, Roy seemed in a joking mood as he exposed himself and told me that was the pipe he needed me to hold. Then he did something he hadn't done yet. He kissed me. He fondled me aggressively, but not like he did when he raped me—the kiss definitely threw me off.

It was my first kiss ever, and his tongue was in my mouth. As he was kissing me with his hands all over me, he backed me up to the cellar wall. My string-tied shorts dropped to the dirt floor as soon as he pulled the string. He put his hand in my underwear and stuck his finger inside of me. After a few seconds, he pushed my panties down. I could feel the coldness and roughness of the poorly-constructed stone and cement cellar wall.

Roy kicked a small piece of wood in front of him and stepped up. I'm guessing he did that because I was a few inches taller than him. His penis penetrated my vagina and this time it didn't hurt, unlike the first two times. He kissed me the entire time and even groaned in pleasure.

Everything happened quickly with Roy. From the time I got into the cellar, to the rape, to back upstairs probably took less than ten minutes, although it felt like an eternity to me.

After he was done, he stepped back and pulled his pants up.

"Thanks, I'm done. You can go back upstairs if you want," he said.

I wiped my face with my shirt to get his alcohol and smoky breath off my skin. I pulled my pants and underwear up and headed upstairs.

"You want to go shoot the gun," he said when I was almost at the top. I didn't know how to answer that question.

"I don't care," I replied. The cellar door was in the kitchen and as I opened it up, all five of his girls were staring at me like they had just seen a ghost. They looked terrified. Did they know what their dad was doing to me? I headed straight to the bathroom as I could feel my panties sticking to me because they were wet. This time, there was no blood.

Roy came up the stairs and told the girls to go outside. By this time, the rain had let up and it was just chilly and wet. Roy grabbed his gun and I followed him outside. I shot it a few times, and he made comments alluding to my fingerprints being on the gun.

He even told me to pull the trigger harder, smirking like 'what are you going to do' the entire time. At one point, Roy grabbed my other hand and placed it on top of the gun and squeezed my fingertips where he knew they would be imprinted.

After firing off a few rounds, we collectively decided to go back inside. It was too cold for us. Roy called us a few sissy names, but went inside as well and continued drinking. I fed everyone lunch and, unlike every other time I babysat, the girls were not forced upstairs to take a nap. I guess because Roy had already raped me, they were off the hook. I wasn't about to object to that, even though their presence had no bearing on his actions.

A couple hours later, my mom and Dawn made it back from Bingo, unfortunately with no jackpot. As soon as my mom stepped in the house, Roy ordered Mary to get her a beer. My mom stayed for her one beer to drink with Roy while they chatted about life. He appeared so ordinary around her. I felt like blurting out what had happened earlier, but no happy ending seemed possible. I couldn't wait to leave, which was exactly what we did once she finished her beer.

The Week After That

On Monday morning, I woke up bleeding; I had started my period. I hadn't even thought about the possibility of getting pregnant until it came on. It did seem a little lighter than normal, which I was completely okay with. I enjoyed the fact that it wasn't so heavy this time. I packed my bag with some supplies and waited on Roy to pick me up. He was a timely guy, never late on picking me up.

"What's in the bag," he asked immediately as I got in his van.

"Oh, it's stuff for my period," I answered, not sure if I should have told him that personal information.

"So you're bleeding this week," he said jokingly. I smirked at the way he said it, but I kept quiet until we got to his house.

As soon as we walked in, all the girls wanted to know what was in the bag. Dawn saw the look on my face and told the girls to stop. We both knew what was in the bag. The girls listened to their mother, and she left for work. I was glad it was nice outside because I wanted the girls to play with each other so I could relax. After all, it was the first day of my period and I didn't feel like doing much.

I took a seat on the picnic table and Amy joined me. We were watching the clouds roll by before we started chatting.

"So, what exactly does your dad do?" I asked her.

"Well, he goes through the border to Canada, drives to the bakery there, picks up some bread and donuts, comes back across the border, and knocks on people's door to see if they want to buy some stuff," she spit it all out.

"Do people actually buy what he sells?" I questioned.

"Sometimes," she said. Amy was such a good girl. She was my favorite of the five of them; maybe it was because we were so close in age. She seemed very mature for eleven.

She continued, "I think he's got to find another job. I heard my mom telling him that and then he got really angry."

"Do they fight a lot," I asked her.

"Not really; my dad is just really, really mean," she said, stressing the two *really*s.

"Does he hit you guys or your mom?" I don't know why I asked the questions I was asked; I guess I was curious to know more about his character.

"He's hit all of us, especially when he's drunk," she replied, not ashamed of any of it. His abuse was a normal part of her life.

"Yea, I noticed he likes to drink a lot," I was agreeing with her because every time I saw him, he had a beer in his hand.

"Every night," she answered, as she got up to go help her sister pull her overloaded wagon of dirt. Amy was so much like her mom—and as sweet as she could be with her younger siblings.

It turned out to be a great week. Roy did not come home one time. Maybe the fact that I was on my period grossed him out, even though I only bled lightly for three days. I wondered if I could tell him every week I was bleeding so that I could escape being raped. All I knew was that it was Friday, also known as my pay day. I had already told my mom that I wanted to stay at home for the weekend, so she should not make plans with

Dawn to go to Bingo. She didn't question my request, and she said she would honor my wishes. I had the whole weekend to myself. I didn't do a thing, but I was happy to have space from the busyness of Dawn and Roy's. I needed that.

Making up for Lost Time

Monday rolled around, and, like clockwork, Roy was in my driveway at 7:30 a.m. to pick me up. I jumped in the van and instantly noticed his angry demeanor. I didn't speak to him and he did not say a word to me. I was confused. *What happened*, I wondered? Eight thousand thoughts ran through my head. Was he mad at me? I didn't have much time to rack my brain, as I was about to be dropped off at the house. I got out without saying a word, and Roy peeled off in his van.

When I walked into the house, Dawn's face looked really puffy, like she had been crying. She told me to feed the girls sandwiches for lunch and rushed out the door. The girls were all sitting at the table with breakfast still on their plate. Everyone looked so sad.

"What's wrong with you guys?" I immediately questioned. Nobody wanted to talk, as they all sat silently at the kitchen table.

Amy finally chimed in. "Dad got really drunk last night and beat Rachel up really bad because she said his breath smelt like liquor."

I directed my attention toward Rachel, who was the quietest out of the five girls and had a slight learning disability. "Are you okay?" I asked.

She shrugged her shoulders with no response to my question, and tears streamed down her face. I could see the side of her forehead was black and blue. I walked closer to her to get a better look.

"You want a cold rag for your head," I offered her. Rachel shook her head yes and it kind of broke the sadness that consumed the house. I grabbed a hand towel out of the bathroom and ran it under the cold water. I rinsed it out the best I could and pressed it against her head. I held it there for a good five minutes before she said she didn't want it there anymore.

"I'm so sorry you guys had to go through that," I said sympathetically. "Let's go outside and play kickball." All five girls hurried to get their sneakers on and out the door we went. We stayed out until lunch time. I had to call a time out from playing ball so I could get their lunch prepared. As soon as I was done, I called for the girls to come in to eat. All five of them ate and asked for a second sandwich, which I made for them. We had played hard. Right after they finished, they all headed upstairs for a nap without me having to say anything. I too considered laying down to take a nap with the girls.

Just as I was cleaning up, I heard a vehicle pull in. My stomach knotted up instantly. Peeking out the window, I saw Roy's van in the driveway. "Shit, he's home," I whispered under my breath. Panic had set in and I was now on high alert.

Roy walked in the house with a loaf of bread in his hand, which he threw on the table.

"What's going on?" he asked.

"Nothing, I just fed the girls their lunch and they were so tired they went upstairs for a nap," I replied. As I talked, he walked towards me. As soon as I finished my sentence, his tongue was in my mouth and his hands were all over every inch of my body.

"Let's go upstairs," he whispered.

"I don't want to do that," I whispered back, completely petrified of him.

"Yea, come on," he said as he took my hand and started leading me up the stairs with a firm grip on my hand. I followed him up the stairs, about to throw up because I knew what was coming. He led me into his bedroom with his hand still holding mine. He let go once we were inside and shut the door behind him. He took his pants off and then unbuckled mine. They dropped to the floor and he pushed me slightly to the side, where I stepped out of my bottoms. He then picked my shirt up over my head. 'Why was I getting completely naked?' I wondered but didn't say a word. He unsnapped my bra in the back and slid my bra straps down my arms. I stood there stiff as a board in utter humiliation.

"Oh, that's nice," he said, examining every inch of my body. I wanted to die I was so embarrassed. To me, there was not one thing nice on any part of my body.

"Lay down," he whispered. I didn't want to, but with the beat down Rachel got the night before, I didn't want to piss him off. As I laid down, he grabbed one leg and pushed it up behind my knee. I had no idea that he was going to lick my private area, but that's exactly what he did. I was so embarrassed that he had a full view of my entire body. He stayed down there for nearly five minutes, and then got on top of me to rape me. Once he got near my face, he kissed me. I could smell my vagina mixed in with his cigarette tainted breath. I tried turning my head to avoid the kiss, but he wasn't having that today. One minute later, he was done.

He got up and put his pants back on. I got up and started dressing. He watched me put on my clothes, which was just another way to make me feel ashamed and humiliated. When I was done, he opened the door to go downstairs and I followed him.

"Can you make me a couple sandwiches?" he asked, like what we had just done was normal. I said nothing as I got the stuff out to make him his sandwiches.

After he wolfed down his sandwiches, he asked me if I was okay, to which I softly replied a yea. I was anesthetized and scared. Nothing about what happened was okay, yet Roy seemed perfectly fine with his action. I felt powerless and completely defeated—again.

Then he kissed me on the mouth and walked out the door to go back to work. I was confused by his behavior, but couldn't really focus on that because my underwear felt wet and soggy. I went into the bathroom and dealt with my reoccurring problem. Why I didn't bring a change of underwear stumped me.

Minutes later, I heard Mary ask if they could get up now. I yelled back that they could. The girls knew what their dad was doing, but nobody dared to speak of it. I felt really sorry for them having to know this information and keep it bottled up inside. I was living their same nightmare, although I definitely thought mine was worse.

For the rest of the week, Roy came home every day to rape me. It was the same scenario daily. He came home for lunch, raped me and back to work he went. The sad part was it didn't matter if the girls were asleep or not. Nobody, not even I, was going to confront him about being a pedophile and a predator.

And, for the most part, I didn't object to his advances. I was too frightened of him.

It was never easy to be naked in front of him, but a part of him grew on me. The more we had sex, the less I fought him. I started to think that Roy actually loved me a little bit. I didn't want to say the same for me, but I was slowly breaking down.

The roughest part about being abused daily was having to face Dawn. My heart ached with every conversation because she honestly had no idea what her husband was doing to me.

My First Love

"Your mom and I are going to Bingo tonight. Any chance you could stay until we get back?" Because it was Dawn who asked me, I couldn't say *no*.

"Sure," I said, but deep down inside I really did not want to stay. She handed me my weekly pay with an extra few dollars for the Friday night service.

Roy arrived home shortly thereafter with a small, blue, rusted truck following him into the driveway. I heard some loud talking and looked outside to see what was going on. There were two (as I could tell) teenage boys outside with him. I will be the first to admit, my heart skipped a beat when I laid my eyes on one of them.

The girls ran outside when they heard the commotion. Mary hurried back into the house to grab three beers.

"Dad told me to tell you to come outside," Mary said to me.

I followed her out and immediately locked eyes with the one that made my heart skip.

"Becky, this is Brian and Brice," Roy said pointing to each of them as he said their name. "These are my first cousins."

"Hi, nice to meet you," I nodded.

"Yowza, you are one hot young lady," Brice chimed in. I immediately blushed and then burst out laughing. It felt good to laugh, something I felt like I hadn't done in ages.

"Roy, how come you didn't tell me the babysitter was this hot?" he questioned like I wasn't standing right in front of him.

"You slick bastard. You thought you could keep all that to yourself," Brice was so bold, but his comment immediately had me thinking that he knew Roy was raping me.

"What?" I questioned his comment.

"Do you have a boyfriend?" Brice asked me, with his curly brown-haired head cocked to the side and his big brown eyes as wide as tennis balls.

"No," I said, with half a smile and butterflies in my stomach because I was smitten with this young man.

"Will you marry me?" Brice asked. Once he said it, everyone erupted in laughter. Roy and Brian questioned his drunkenness. Brice defended his question by telling everyone he was in love—it was love at first sight.

"I'm only fifteen," I said to him.

"Well, I'm only eighteen," he replied back like that was supposed to make it okay to get married.

I had to catch my bearing. If he was serious, I felt the same connection. Even though I was fifteen, I was smitten with Brice from his looks alone. Brice wasn't that tall, but he was a husky guy. His hair was messy like it hadn't been combed in a day, but I think that added to his charm. He had full lips and perfectly straight teeth. His personality set him apart from anyone I had ever met before.

"You God damn idiot, shut the hell up," Roy chimed in. I noticed Roy was agitated by Brice's focused attention on me.

Just then, my mom drove up in the driveway. Dawn came out of the house and headed toward the picnic table, which we were all gathered around. Roy introduced the boys to my mom and they all talked for a few minutes. Before they left for Bingo, Dawn gave some specific instructions, like you better not be drinking and driving and they better not get too drunk, but they laughed as she handed out some motherly advice.

Roy asked me to go get them some more beer. As I got up to go in the house, he made a comment about my large frame and ass. I was completely embarrassed and kept walking like I didn't hear it. That's when Brice stated he couldn't wait for me to be his wife so he could have all of it. I smiled, but Roy went off about what an idiot he was for even thinking about marrying me.

I was on cloud nine for the rest of the evening hanging out with Brice. Brice had nothing but nice things to say to me and about me. Roy was pretty sauced, so I think he let things go after a while. By the time my mom and Dawn got home three hours later, I knew I was in love with Brice.

My mom came over to the picnic table and said it was time to go. Brice begged me for my number. I couldn't help but laugh. He had consumed enough beer to fill a small pond but said he didn't need a piece of paper to remember my phone number. My mom laughed as she said I could give it to him, but not to be sad if he didn't call. Brice had really made a spectacle of himself by calling her "Mom."

I left Roy and Dawn's that night, so happy that I stayed. My mom didn't like the fact that Brice drank so much, but she was not going to chastise me about it. I think she was happy to see me laugh and have fun. I had never hung out with boys, let alone been with one that showed interest in me. My world had changed in an instant. I was crazy about Brice.

Our phone rang the next morning. Butterflies immediately hit my stomach. I knew in my heart that it was Brice, and I was right. I couldn't believe it. He kept his word… and remembered my number even though he was really drunk.

"Hey Becky, how's it going?" he asked.

"Good, how are you feeling," surely he had to be hung over. I was laughing.

"I'm great now that I've heard your voice." Brice surely knew how to make me feel good. My response was more laughter.

"You busy tonight? Can I take you out?" he asked.

"I'll have to check with my mom first, but I'm sure she'll let me," I responded.

"Well, go ask," he said. I laughed some more and told him to hold on while I set the phone down. I quickly told my mom that Brice was on the phone wanting to know if I could go out with him tonight. She didn't have a problem with it and seemed kind of happy someone finally asked me out.

"I can go," I said when I picked the phone back up.

"You live right there on Route 41 across from the Wilsons' farm right?"

"Yes," I said, but I wondered in my head how he knew where I lived. Like he could read my mind, he told me Roy had told him where I lived. Apparently, I was a hot topic after I left the house. At that point, I really didn't care. I just wanted to go out with Brice.

I asked him a few questions regarding our date for the night. Brice said he didn't know what we were going to do other than be together. He told me I could plan whatever I wanted and he would make it happen. Brice had to work on the family farm and wouldn't be done doing chores in the barn until about 8 p.m., but said he'd be at my house no later than 8:30.

He was on time, sober, and looking like he had just won the jackpot when he showed up at my house. I invited him in and introduced him to my dad and sister. My mom had met him at Dawn and Roy's the previous night, so she did not need an introduction. She questioned him about where we were going and what we had planned. He had an answer for everything even though he never quite answered one question. Brice was quick witted and funny.

My mom let us leave with no concrete plan, and my dad was glued to the television like always. Brice told my mom he needed to go eat, but that was the extent of our evening plans. We left for our date and headed straight to the local ice cream stand, which also served food. He placed his order and we waited until they called our number. I got ice cream and enjoyed that while he wolfed his food down like he had been starved for the last six months. It didn't bother me that he ate so much or so fast, I just wanted to be with him.

After we left the Tasty-Freeze, Brice asked if I wanted to go hang out at the lake. I asked if there was a party or people he was supposed to meet. He said no, that it was just him. I laughed at his answer and was relieved. I did not want to be around a bunch of people. That wasn't my style; I avoided social interaction as much as possible.

We arrived at the lake and Brice parked his blue and white 1969 Ford LTD. The moon was so big and bright that night. We talked about everything that night, including Roy, but not the fact that he had raped me multiple times. The more we talked, the more I knew that Roy had not told him his dirty little secret. That night, I felt more loved than I ever had in my entire life. Brice was so comical and goofy, yet such a gentleman. It was obvious that he was really interested in me.

It was near midnight and I had to tell him that I had to get back home. We left our peaceful spot on the lake and Brice drove me home. When we arrived at my house, he leaned over and kissed me on the mouth. My heart melted.

"Can I call you tomorrow?" he asked as I was getting out of the car.

"Sure," I said, my whole body still tingling from the kiss.

I went to bed that night unable to sleep. I was in love with Roy's cousin. The next morning, I heard the phone ring and my mom say I was still asleep. I raced out of the bed to stop her, but she hung up the phone that quickly.

"Mom," I said with a disappointing tone.

"Well honey, I'm sorry, I thought you were still asleep. He said he'll call you back later," she replied. "How was your date?"

"Amazing," I said, "I think I'm in love."

My mom laughed out loud but said nothing.

I sat by the phone all day waiting for him to call back. He finally called right before he was getting ready to go do chores. I was so happy to hear his voice.

"Can I see you after I get done chores?" he asked.

"Sure," I said, trying to keep my emotions in check.

"Okay, I'll see you in a little bit then," he told me.

"Okay, bye," I said, not wanting to hang up the phone, but doing so anyway.

Around 8:30 p.m., I heard his car pull into the driveway. I went outside to meet him and was greeted with the most romantic and sweetest hug and a kiss. *How is this guy this awesome*, I silently wondered.

He asked me if I could go grab something to eat with him and what time I had to be back. I checked with my parents, and this time they said I could go, but I had to be back by 10 p.m. because I had to babysit in the morning. I was fine with their decision. I didn't care what we did or where we went, I just wanted to be with Brice.

We left my house and headed straight to the Tasty-Freeze, the same place as the night before. Brice ordered the same exact meal and I ordered ice cream. After he ate, we headed to the same spot on the lake. It wasn't as nice as the night before, but I didn't care—I was with my man.

This night solidified the bond we had, as Brice asked me to be his girlfriend. I graciously accepted and was so in love with him. Brice was a perfect gentleman. We kissed that night, but by no means did he cross the line with anything inappropriate. The only thing he took was my breath away. Brice stole my heart.

He brought me home that night and I shared everything with my mom. She was happy that I was happy. I don't know if she had the same experience with my dad. If she did, she didn't share it with me. She had no advice or guidance to offer. I was on my own to figure it all out.

Everything about Brice screamed that he was the one in my young immature teenaged mind. I fantasized about him when I went to bed that night. I saw us getting married and being so happy together. It was wonderful having these thoughts, but the reality of my situation was that I had to work the next morning.

I was scared about how Roy would handle the news that I was Brice's girlfriend, but it was done and I wasn't going to change it.

Sharing my New Status

Roy picked me up the next morning. He seemed a little pissed off, but I had not said a word.

"You go out with Brice this weekend," he questioned with an angry tone.

"Yes," I said, sensing his irritation over Brice's and my status.

"Brian told me. So, what's the deal? What's up with you two?" he was pissed.

"We're going out, Roy. Brice is my boyfriend," I replied matter-of-factly, albeit with some hesitation.

"That's freaking wonderful... just freaking wonderful!" He pulled into the driveway, obviously not happy with my announcement, and I jumped out of the van. I walked into the house, where Dawn was going through her normal routine of getting ready for work. We made some small talk about Brice and me, and she confessed that Brice was her favorite out of all the boys.

Unfortunately, because of our work schedules, Brice and I would only be able to see each other on the weekends. We had to resort to a few short phone calls during the week. I lived for those calls, and the work week couldn't go by fast enough. For me, having Brice in my life almost made me forget about the craziness I was going through with Roy.

The week had flown by at Roy and Dawn's. I made it to Friday, without incident. Just when I felt free from Roy, I heard his van pull in the driveway. I had already sent the girls upstairs for a nap.

'Oh my God, he knows I'm Brice's' girlfriend, surely he's not home to rape me' was all I could think. Plus, I knew my phone call from Brice was coming within the next thirty minutes while he was on his lunch break.

As soon as Roy walked in the door, he said hey as he walked toward me. He grabbed me aggressively and slobbered across my neck. He sucked it ever so slightly and asked me what Brice would think if he saw a hickey on my neck.

"Roy, please don't, please stop, I don't want to do this," I pleaded with him.

"Well give me what I want and you don't have to worry about me saying anything," he heartlessly demanded. "Let's go upstairs."

By then, tears were pouring down my face. I did not want to be with Roy ever again. I had Brice, and I only wanted to be with him.

"Wipe your face, you big baby," he commanded firmly, pushing me toward the stairs. "Get up there right now, I ain't got much time."

I took two steps and pleaded, "Please don't do this. I just don't want to do this anymore."

He grabbed my face and squished it tightly. "I don't give a shit what you want. Get your fat ass up there right now."

There was no denying his demand. My fear was justified. I slowly walked up the stairs and could hear Amy and Tara talking in the bed. When they heard our feet, Amy told Tara to be quiet. I walked into Roy and Dawn's bedroom. Roy immediately dropped his pants, revealing that he was fully erect. He grabbed my shorts and pushed them down around my ankles. He tripped me back onto the bed and got on top of me. He tried to kiss me as he entered me, but I turned my head. I did not ever want to kiss him and I was pissed that this was even happening when he knew I had a boyfriend. After he was done, he told me to get my ass downstairs and make him some lunch. Without saying a word, I did exactly as he said. As he ate his lunch, the phone rang. It was Brice.

"Hey baby, whatcha doing?" Brice asked, not having a clue how traumatized I was after having just had sex with Roy. Roy was in the background, gesturing that I not let Brice know he was home.

"Oh nothing, just getting ready to eat lunch," I replied.

"Oh yah, whatcha having?" he questioned.

"Just a sandwich… hey Brice, can I call you back in a minute? I need to go check on the girls because I think I heard them talking and they are supposed to be asleep," I said because I could see the steam coming off Roy's head because I was talking to Brice. He was pissed and I did not want to piss him off anymore.

"Sure, call me back when you're done. I have to go back into the field in about ten minutes, though."

"Oh, okay," I said like it was going to take me more than ten minutes to check on the girls.

"Hey, just stay at Roy and Dawn's tonight. I'm going over there after I get done chores to have a few beers," he stated.

Deep down, I was dying inside. "Okay, I'll see you later on tonight." I hung up the phone. I hated the fact that Roy was going to watch me interact with Brice. I knew Roy hated that I had the feelings I had towards him. His body language and attitude clearly told me so.

Ten minutes after I got off the phone, Roy left to go back to work. It was almost as if he purposely stayed so I wouldn't have time to call Brice back before he had to go back into the field. It angered me more than anything. No sooner than my frustration consumed me, guilt crept in because I had, in my mind, cheated on Brice. I shut down. The only thing that snapped me back to reality was the girls calling to ask if they could get up.

For the rest of the afternoon, my brain did not rest. I desperately needed to figure out how I could stop Roy from raping me. I did not want to lose Brice because of Roy's impulsive behavior.

I took the girls outside to play, and, before I knew it, Dawn was pulling into the driveway. She handed me my weekly pay and offered me a ride home. I let her know that I would be staying because Brice was coming over. I wanted to have alone time with Brice, but I was going to do whatever he wanted. She was completely fine with the idea and headed into the house to start dinner.

Within thirty minutes of her arrival, Roy came home. He glared at me like he was ready to fight. I stared him down. What could he do to me with Dawn at home? I knew I would pay for my actions, but in my mind, I would kick his ass if he tried to rape me again. I had a plan to kick him in his erect penis and then punch him in his face when he bent over. After I punched him, I was going to knee him as hard as I could in the face. I hoped to at least break his nose. And then, after I beat the shit out of him, I would tell everyone what he did to me all summer.

Roy went into the house while we all stayed outside. Dawn called us in a little later to eat dinner. It was awkward eating with them because I always felt like Roy was watching how much I ate, but I made it through and helped Dawn clean up the kitchen. The only thing I had left to do was wait for my honey to show up.

It was exactly 8:30 p.m. when Brice pulled in. He had already been drinking and seemed a little buzzed, but I didn't care. He was so affectionate toward me, and that was all I wanted. He held my hand and caressed my hair all night in front of Roy. I was nervous watching Roy get hammered because I didn't know if he'd say anything stupid; I would have died if Brice found out about us. After Brice was done hanging out with Roy, he asked me if I wanted a ride home. Of course, I did because I wanted to spend every second of every day with him.

Brice and I got ready to leave Roy and Dawn's. Before we left, Dawn fussed at Brice about drinking and driving but didn't try to stop us. I think Roy and his cousins all drove drunk so often that she was not fazed by it. I guess because I was leaving with him, she told Brice to be careful.

We didn't make it too far up the road before Brice asked me if I want to chat for a while. I said yes, of course. He stopped his car on the side of the road and turned it off. Our talking soon turned to kissing. I felt Brice's hand caress my breast. That was the first time he had ever felt anything on me. I let him do it, wanting to give Brice all of me, but I couldn't because Roy had raped me earlier in the day. I did not want to have sex with two different men on the same day, even though the sex with Roy was not consensual.

As Brice's hand dropped from my breast to the button on my jeans, I told him that I didn't want to do anything more than kiss. He honored my request, which made me think Brice was the greatest guy ever. We continued to make out for a few more minutes and then I asked him to take me home. Brice started his car and did just that. He truly was my knight in shining armor.

He dropped me off at home, and we made our plans for Saturday night. How could I deal with Roy raping me when all I wanted to do was give Brice all of me? At fifteen, I was completely and utterly confused.

The next evening, Brice showed up at his usual time and we headed to the Tasty-Freeze so he could eat. Once again, I had ice cream. I was already a big girl, but I loved ice cream. After he ate, we went to the lake to hang out. Brice asked me if I wanted to go to the movies or roller skating, but I didn't want to do anything where we would not have each other's full attention. Plus, I hated crowds. I always felt like people stared at me because of my physical appearance.

We ended our Saturday night with the usual kiss and planned out our Sunday. Sunday was the same scenario. Brice picked me up, he ate dinner and I ate ice cream. We went to the lake and spent our few precious hours together, talking and making out. He always made sure I was home before curfew. I never wanted our time together to end, but unfortunately, I had to work, as did he, the next morning.

Caught in the Act

      I didn't feel well when I woke up, but got up anyway to get ready to go to Roy and Dawn's to babysit. They relied on me to do my job so they could do theirs, plus I needed the money. I didn't know what was wrong, but I guessed that it was the ice cream I had with Brice the night before. I ate it two nights in a row.

Roy was there to pick me up promptly at 7:30 in the morning. Immediately he asked me what was wrong as I sluggishly got in the van. I told him I didn't feel well, to which he replied, "Are you pregnant?"

Those words penetrated every cell in my body. I actually tingled when he said it.

"No, I think it was the ice cream I had yesterday," I replied.

"Like your fat ass needs some ice cream," he commented, not knowing, nor caring, that his words cut me like a knife.

Today of all days he had to belittle me. I didn't feel well and was making an effort to do my job, and this was the thanks that I got. His comment angered me so much that I wanted to quit right there on the spot.

As if he could read my mind, he said, "You know Dawn really likes you. When the girls have school breaks, she wants you to babysit."

"Oh," I replied. I knew that once I left, I was never coming back. I didn't even want to finish out the summer, let alone come back during school breaks.

Roy dropped me off at the house. When I was getting out, he said he'd see me later. I turned to look at him to see if he meant *see me later* to rape me or *see me later* like tomorrow to babysit. His smirk spoke volumes as I slammed the door.

More than anything, all I wanted to do was be with Brice. It seemed like the closer Brice and I got, the madder Roy was with our relationship. He had so much power over me and I was sick of it.

Dawn left for work and the girls and I hung around inside the house because of the weather. Right after I sent them upstairs for a nap, I heard Roy's van pull in. *That son of a bitch*, I thought. I don't know what was wrong with me that day, whether it was just because I wasn't feeling well or because I was fed up with his attacks, but I did not feel like being raped. I felt like today was going to be the day that I implemented the attack I had fantasized about.

Roy came in the house and ordered me upstairs immediately. I told him *no*. I still didn't feel good and I wasn't going upstairs. He grabbed my arm tightly and got in my face.

"What the hell do you think you're doing? You don't get to tell me *no*! Who the hell do you think you are? Now get your ass up those steps right now, or you'll regret it." His teeth were clenched together while he said all this. In reality, he looked possessed. Out of pure fear for my life, I went upstairs. It was eerily quiet. Maybe all the girls were actually asleep.

Roy shoved me in the bedroom and closed the door. He slipped his pants down and grabbed the tie string to my shorts. They fell to the floor and I went to grab them.

"No," I said, resisting firmly and in my regular voice. I was not whispering, not that day.

Roy grabbed my face and squeezed really hard. "You don't tell me *no*," he whispered viciously.

"Let me go," I said out loud and was staring him down. I had enough of him already. Roy flung me around and I hit the floor with both knees.

"Stop it," I cried, trying to get up to secure my shorts.

Just then, Tara busted in the bedroom door. I still hadn't made it off the floor completely, and her father stood there completely exposed. The look on her face told a story like no other. Roy took three steps forward, pushed her out of the room and slammed the door in her face.

"Look what you did," he said, pulling his pants up. After he got his belt secure, he tried to pick me up by my arm off the floor. "Go beat her ass," he demanded.

"What?" I was confused as I looked at him, and my knees collapsed back onto the floor.

"I said, 'Go beat her ass,'" his orders were clear, but my brain did not comprehend what he was ordering me to do. He wanted me to go beat his daughter because he was trying to rape me and I resisted? There was no logic in his reasoning. By this time, my arms were black and blue from his grab, my face was red from his squeeze and my knees were throbbing from hitting the floor. Now he wanted me to discipline a child that was trying to save me.

I took too long to respond to his demand. Roy grabbed a handful of hair and pulled as hard as he could. I rose to my feet but remained bent over. I tried grabbing his forearm to release some of the pain, but it was not working.

Roy got down in my face and said, "If you don't your ass out there right now and beat the shit out of Tara, I will kill you and your family tonight. Do you understand me?"

I couldn't shake my head because he was still pulling my hair. Instead, I mustered up a soft *yes*, and at that moment, he shoved my head to the side and let go of my hair. He grabbed a belt that was hanging on a nail in the frame of the door and threw it on the bed.

"Use this," he ordered. He walked out and ordered Amy out of the bedroom. She hurried out and he kicked her as she went by him. She let out a painful yelp but didn't look back as she entered the bedroom where her three other siblings were.

I feared for Tara's life because of the way Roy was glaring at her. If looks could kill, she would have been dead instantly. In that moment, I felt so helpless and hopeless. Why did she have to come in? Why did she see what was happening? Was she sticking up for me or defying her father?

Regardless, I cried as I walked across the hall with the belt in my hand. As he turned to walk down the stairs, he looked coldly in my eyes and said, "If she doesn't scream, I'm coming back up here." With that, he left me standing there, traumatized that I was going to have to inflict pain on his daughter.

I looked at Tara, and she was paralyzed with fear. My anger and rage kicked in along with the lingering questions that I asked myself minutes earlier. I was pissed she saw us half naked. I was pissed her father had repeatedly raped me over the last eight weeks. I was pissed that I was powerless to change my circumstances. I lifted the belt and unleashed the first lick across her back and butt, and I continued to whip her with such force that she was screaming and begging me to stop. The beating lasted a good three minutes. Tara's face was as red as a tomato and wet with tears and slobber. The way she looked at me, I knew I had scarred this child for life. My heart was cut deep as I threw the belt on the bed and walked out.

As I walked by the other bedroom, I could hear the other four girls weeping as quietly as they could. I did not want to face them and, I'm sure they felt the same. With the paper-thin walls in the house, there is no doubt they heard everything. I had never felt so ashamed in my life. That day, I resigned to quit. I literally could not take it another day!

I went downstairs, besieged with feelings of worthlessness and remorse. Roy glared at me with hatred in his eyes and walked out the door to go back to work. I went into the bathroom and broke down. I sobbed uncontrollably for a good thirty minutes. After I was done, I yelled upstairs to the girls that they could come down. Nobody moved. I had never felt more rejected in my life.

After about fifteen minutes of them remaining upstairs, panic set in. How could I possibly tell Dawn that I beat her child? What excuse could I give her? Do I say nothing and pray that no one tells? The stress of the whole situation sent me into a full-fledged anxiety attack.

I had the phone in my hand to dial 911. My fingers wouldn't push the numbers. I felt like I was going to die, yet there was no way I could explain what was really going on. Would I go to jail because I abused a child? Would Roy kill me and my family as planned? What would Dawn think of me? Never once did it register to me that Roy could have gone to jail for raping me or ordering me to physically harm his daughter.

I was completely incapable of handling the magnitude of the situation. Do I go upstairs and apologize? Do I let all the girls be angry? Do I force them downstairs? How was I supposed to act towards them when I had just abused their sister? About an hour or so later, I heard all five girls slowly coming down the stairs. Samantha was the first one to speak and asked if they could have a snack. I got some milk and crackers out and placed them on the table. All five girls ate, but nobody said a word. I had never felt more hated in my life as I felt that day. I knew once I left for the day, there was no way I would return to the house of horror.

I'm Pregnant, Now What?

Dawn came home that afternoon to a somber atmosphere. Obviously, she asked questions, but nobody would say a word. She was trying to guess, but her speculations were obviously wrong. Dawn started to become angry and demanded to know what happened. I was frozen in fear because I had never seen Dawn so adamant. Amy, in an instant, chimed in.

"Tara and I got in a fight today," Amy totally lied, but it sounded like music to my ears. A rush of relief came over me like a gentle breeze.

"About what," Dawn over exasperated her tone.

"Well, Tara wanted to watch cartoons so she snatched the remote out of my hands and it hit me the chin, which hurt, so I punched her." All eyes were captivated on Amy as she spoke. I could tell Tara desperately wanted to tell the truth, but there was no way she was going to risk her life at her father's hands. How Amy came up with her story so quickly was beyond me, but I admired her quick wit at such a young age.

"Oh, my God! You two know better than to fight! I may have to tell your father when he gets home." Dawn was pissed, but even in anger, her temperament was soft. As Dawn fussed, I could sense a relief amongst all of the girls, myself included, that she actually believed Amy's story.

"Becky, I am so sorry you had to put up with that today! I can assure you that this will not happen again!" Dawn spoke firmly, looking at the two girls.

"It's okay Dawn. I love these girls," I said, hoping to hear them say something, anything to know they weren't mad at me anymore. All five of them sat there stone-faced and nobody said a word. I could feel my emotions well up inside and did my best to fight back the tears.

"You ready to go home," Dawn asked.

"Yea, I'm ready," I replied, as I grabbed my jacket.

"Is everything okay?" Dawn questioned.

"Yea, I just don't feel good today," I told her as we got in the car.

As soon as I got home, I headed straight to my bedroom and sobbed uncontrollably all over again. How was I going to get out of this situation? My thoughts consumed me. I wanted to die, my anguish was so great.

I don't know how I fell asleep in my bed with all that was going on, but my mom came into my room to let me know Brice was on the phone. I crawled out of bed to get my time in with him. We didn't talk about anything special; I just loved hearing his voice. We made plans to see each other Friday night at Roy and Dawn's. I hated it, but what was I going to say? By no means did I want anyone to know what Roy had been doing to me.

After I got off the phone with Brice, I chatted a while with my mom, dad and sister. It felt good to be around them, especially with the day that I had. In our conversation, I asked my mom if she thought it would be okay for me to take a couple days off from babysitting so we could go shopping for school.

My mom told me to run it by Dawn to see if she would be able to get some time off. I was trying to find any excuse I could so I would never have to return to their house again, but I knew that I would be going back. I thought about calling Dawn that evening but never got around to it. Actually, I didn't have the guts to do it. I was in a predicament! I didn't want to jeopardize seeing Brice at their hands, but I also no longer wanted to be raped. Having to beat Tara messed my entire world up.

I went to bed that night and prayed I wouldn't wake up the next morning. Because I had slept for so long when I got home, I was unsure if I was going to be able to back to sleep. Fortunately for me, I slept like I was knocked out. Unfortunately, I was still alive.

As my alarm clock went off the next morning, I felt like I could have slept for four more hours. I had to force myself out of bed. The more I moved, the more I noticed I wasn't feeling well. I got dressed anyway, thinking and hoping it would eventually go away. Breakfast was the last thing I wanted, plus I had eaten a late dinner. As I walked outside to wait on Roy, I threw up. As he was pulling in, I was hunched over in the driveway puking. I couldn't put all that was happening together.

"What's wrong with you?" Roy asked after he rolled down the window.

"I don't know. I just don't feel good," I replied.

"Well, get in. I don't want Dawn to be late for work," he demanded.

"I don't think I can babysit today," I said, with tears rolling down my face. I was sick as a dog. My body felt nauseous all the way into my toes.

"You'll be alright. You can rest at our house. Come on, get in." Roy was completely unsympathetic.

I slowly walked to the van and got in. I felt like I was going to throw up again the entire ride to the house. Roy did not say a word to me. He dropped me off and kept going. When I got in the house, Dawn took one look at me and immediately asked what was wrong. I told her I wasn't feeling well. She told me that she was going to bring me back home and that she would work out other arrangements for child care. Dawn confessed that Roy was an idiot for even bringing me there.

I got home and went right back to bed. I slept until noon, but I felt better after I woke up. I lazed around the entire day and watched television. I enjoyed my break from babysitting, especially with everything that had happened the day before.

Later on that evening, Dawn called to check on me. Why I didn't lie and tell her I was still sick eludes me to this day. I told her I felt much better and would be available to babysit tomorrow. However, the next morning rolled around, and much like the previous morning, I was sick as a dog.

Before Roy could get to my house, I called Dawn to let her know I was still sick and apologized profusely. I made it back to my bed and slept until noon again. Once I got up, I felt fine. It was great to have another day off, yet I knew my pay was going to suck because I had not worked for two days. I vowed if I was sick again the next morning, I was going to push through because I knew I would be okay eventually. Plus, Brice and I had already committed to meeting at Roy and Dawn's

Friday night. In my mind, there was no way I couldn't work all week and then show up to see my boyfriend.

Dawn called that evening to see how I was doing. I told her I felt better and that she could count on me being there the next morning. Sure enough, the next day Roy was in my driveway at 7:30 a.m. to get me. I was sick as a dog but wanted to keep my word. I also wanted to see if the girls would accept me. I wanted their forgiveness more than anything.

"What the hell is wrong with you?" Roy demanded.

"I have no idea. I'm only sick in the morning and then I'm fine for the rest of the day," I responded, completely oblivious to my own comment.

"Who you been screwing?" Roy questioned.

I was confused by his query, but immediately answered, "No one." Why he asked me that kept going through my mind?

"Brice's coming over Friday night," he said.

"Yea, I know," I replied, unsure of where this conversation was headed. It didn't matter because we were soon at the house, and he dropped me off. I dragged myself into the house, still nauseous but determined to make it through the day. I perked up as best I could so Dawn would not suspect anything. The girls did greet me when I arrived, which melted my heart. I knew it would never be the same between us, but at least they spoke to me.

I made it through the next two days of babysitting. I rested in the morning and by the afternoon I was fine. Friday morning I finally got the guts to pull Tara aside and apologized for what happened. Tara's big brown eyes told me she'd never forget, but she said she forgave me. I knew she wanted to address what she saw, but I never wanted to talk about it again. Tara was the most defiant out of the five girls, and I would have to say, even at age nine, she internalized much of what happened in her life.

Fortunately, Roy didn't come home for lunch or to rape me. I thought maybe what had happened with Tara would change him forever. I hoped he would apologize to her, but deep down, I knew he never would. Roy's cocky and arrogant personality wouldn't allow him to say he was sorry about anything.

That afternoon, Dawn came home from work and said she was going to Bingo. After she paid me, she offered to take me with her, but I told her I had plans with Brice. She had forgotten, but I hadn't. Tara and Amy chimed in that they would like to go, and Dawn agreed to take them. Dawn fixed a quick dinner, and the three of them left right after they ate.

I was alone with Roy and the three younger girls. Dawn hadn't been gone five minutes when Roy ordered the three little ones outside. Fear gripped every inch of my body. I couldn't fathom that this was going to happen right before Brice showed up. Roy looked at me and told me to relax, that he just wanted to talk.

As soon as the girls left out the door, Roy started, "You been screwing Brice?"

"No," I responded, shocked, shaking, and scared stiff.

"You need to screw him tonight," he affirmed to me.

"Roy, I'm not doing that!" I told him.

"Why not? You know you want to," Roy stated matter-of-factly. "Look, I'll leave you alone if you do."

Was Roy negotiating with me? Was he serious? I wanted to believe him, but my gut told me he was lying through his teeth. What was his problem? All these thoughts and emotions were running through my head trying to figure out where he was going with this talk.

"I don't know," I responded, shaking my head no. I really didn't know. My mind was racing a thousand miles a minute.

"I do!" he declared, "And you better get it done tonight!" Just then, Mary popped her head in the door.

"Can we come in?" she asked. She was hands down the cutest of the five and had the best personality.

"I don't care," Roy mumbled. With that, the three of them were back in the house, playing with their toys. Within the hour, Brice pulled in. He'd been drinking, but that was fine by me as long as I got to see him.

We ended up staying in the house because of the weather. Brice was pounding beers left and right. He and Roy drank a twenty-four pack, plus whatever was in the fridge. They were loud and obnoxious with each other, but Brice still managed to focus a little attention on me. He kept his arm around me for most of the evening. I felt like a goddess around him.

After having way too much to drink, Brice wanted to move to the couch. Roy was left at the kitchen table by himself, and the three girls were playing quietly on the kitchen floor. He yelled a few sexual comments into the living room like he wanted us to have sex right there. Roy wasn't making sense, but I assumed it was because they had drunk so much. Brice slurred for him to shut the hell up. Within a couple of minutes, Brice passed out. It's the first time I had ever seen him like that.

Once Dawn and the girls returned from Bingo, she offered to drive me home, which I accepted. Dawn had won a small jackpot of one hundred dollars, so everyone was pretty happy. I guess the fact that both Roy and Brice were stinking drunk didn't faze her; she was probably used to it.

I got home and immediately went to bed. I felt exhausted and ended up sleeping late the next morning. Once I got up and started moving, I was sick again. My mom inquired about what she thought I had going on. I had no idea. She asked me a few questions regarding how serious Brice and I were, which I immediately chimed in that we had not been having sex. I left off the part about me and Roy. I couldn't tell her—I didn't have the courage to divulge that kind of information.

I felt better by the afternoon, but Brice was feeling the pain of his overindulgence. He called to let me know he was sick as a dog, so we'd have to wait until Sunday to see each other. I was devastated. My heart felt like it was broken. I was pitiful and sat in front of the television all day.

Sunday rolled around and once again I was sick. My mother let me know that she would be taking me to the doctors the next day, so I had to call Dawn to inform her that I would not be available to babysit Monday morning. Dawn said she'd make other arrangements and that I would see her on Tuesday.

That evening, Brice came by to get me. I couldn't wait to spend time with him, as I missed him so much the day before. We did our normal routine and headed to the Tasty-Freeze and then to the lake.

Once at the lake, we engaged in some French kissing and heavy petting. Roy's directive to have sex so that he would leave me alone was ringing in my ear. Somehow, I needed to make this happen so I could report it back to Roy and be free of him forever.

Brice was such a gentleman that he kept his hands in 'safe' places. That is, he kept them there until I placed them where I wanted them. He was obviously excited and had to excuse himself from the car. I wondered what he did, but didn't question him. When he got back in the car, we immediately started making out again. This time, I slid my hand over the crotch of his pants. They were wet.

"Sorry, sorry, sorry, I got a little too excited there," he stumbled over his words, but I knew that he meant he had ejaculated in his pants. I laughed at the thought that he was that excited over me. I didn't care. I was in love with Brice.

"I'm ready if you are," I announced.

"Ready for what," Brice was playing with me. He knew darn well what I meant.

"Brice," I said with my head cocked to the side, and serious look on my face. I leaned in and kissed him as passionately as I could. I moved my hand back over the wet spot on his Levi jeans. He was ready, as was I.

Brice's hands moved across my breasts and then down to the button on my jeans. I was not resisting him tonight. After he unbuttoned and unzipped my jeans, I pushed my hand on top of his so that he would go further. I wanted to feel his finger inside of me. I wanted to feel much more, but that would come in time. I didn't want to rush our first time.

As his hand made his way into my jeans, his fingers gently glided into my vagina, sending a tingle through my entire body. I was so wet because I was excited to be with him. I wanted him so badly. I needed to connect with him on that level, and I was hoping he would love me forever. I started to unbutton and unzip his pants as we continued to make out. He was fully erect.

I tried pushing Brice's pants off, but his sitting position made it impossible. Brice paused for just a moment to ask me if I was sure I wanted to do this. I told him *yes*, that I was ready to be his.

We decided to move to the back seat of the car so we could be a little more comfortable. I exited from the passenger's side door while he got out of the driver's side. We both opened the back doors to the car and crawled in. Once we both undressed, I laid down in the back seat. Brice reached over the front seat and grabbed his wallet out of the back pocket of his jeans. He fished around for a moment before he announced that he had some protection.

Brice slipped the condom on and eased his way inside of me. It was great, but it didn't last long. I was okay with that because I was so in love with Brice. After we were done and got dressed, Brice and I talked in the back seat for a while.

"You know, Becky, I think I love you," Brice claimed.

My heart was beating so fast I thought he could hear it. I was ready to marry Brice, despite only having known him for a few short weeks.

"I know I love you, Brice. You give me butterflies every time I see you," I replied back to him.

"No way," he laughed. "Me, I'm just a country boy that ain't got shit."

"You got me for as long as you want," I reassured him. Was this puppy love? Was it real? At that moment, it felt as real as life itself.

We continued to talk until I had to get home before curfew. That Sunday night, I was on top of the world. Little did I know that my life was about to be over the very next day!

I woke up early for my doctor's appointment. I told my mom that I thought we could cancel it because I no longer felt sick. She insisted that we go just to make sure everything was okay.

Once we arrived and got checked in, we waited for the doctor to call us back. Once there, he asked a lot of questions, including whether I was sexually active. My hesitation after that question spoke volumes. He also wanted to know when I had my last cycle. I told him my dates but also included that it was unusually light. With the information he had, the doctor thought it would be best to give me a pregnancy test.

My stomach was in knots and all I could think about was that Brice wore a condom. For whatever reason, sex with Roy wasn't resonating in my mind. As a teenager, I didn't always think rationally. In my mind, I figured because Roy was married and he raped me, I couldn't get pregnant by him. How skewed were my thoughts?

I entered the bathroom and peed in the cup. I went back in the room with my mom, where she looked really anxious. I believe she already knew I was pregnant.

"Mom, I have to tell you something," my whole body was beating, as I was staring blankly at the floor.

"What is it, Becky?" she said, anticipating what I was about to say.

"I had sex with Brice last night," I broke down crying. "We used a condom, but maybe it broke and now I'm pregnant," I said through my sobs.

"Oh Becky, honey, you don't get pregnant overnight. If you were pregnant, you would have had to have sex a few weeks ago. Did you?" my mom asked.

Right when I shook my head *no*, the doctor was back in the room with a funny look on his face.

"Becky, you're pregnant," he stated boldly. I didn't hear anything he said after that. He was talking, but I had entered into a state of shock. My mother was answering the questions he asked. I literally could not speak.

The next thing I remember is being in my mom's car with her questioning how long Brice and I had been screwing and why we weren't careful. She was going on and on and on about Brice. I finally exploded, "It wasn't Brice. It was Roy!"

Silence gripped the air as she drove us home. I was in shock, as was she. My mom walked into the house, zombie-like. For the next few hours, we said nothing. We just cried and cried some more.

The Secret is Out

"Becky, we have to talk about this," my mom insisted with tears streaming down her face.

"I'm so sorry, Mommy. I'm sorry," I sobbed uncontrollably.

"Becky, what happened? What do you mean 'it was Roy'?" my mom asked.

"Roy came onto me and made me have sex with him," I said.

"You mean he raped you?" my mom asked.

I shrugged my shoulders, as if to say *I don't know*, and continued to cry.

"How long has this been going on?" she questioned.

"All summer," I blurted out.

I could not only see my mother's anguish; I could feel it within my body.

"We have to call the police," my mom was headed towards the phone.

"No mom, we can't call the police," I said emphatically. Panic had set in, and the situation had spiraled out of control. I was so heavy with the all the decisions that not only needed to be made but would affect the rest of my life.

"Becky, tell me what's going on," she pleaded.

I trembled with fear. "Mom, I'm sorry. I'm so sorry. What have I done?" Sobbing through my reality, I told my mom that Roy had forced himself on me, but minimized the brutality and number of times it happened. I tried to lessen the viciousness of the crime with a simple 'we had sex' vibe to it.

"I'm calling Dawn right now," my mother wanted her to know what a piece of shit husband she was dealing with.

"No, please don't call Dawn. Mom, please," I pleaded, "I can't do this right now."

"What the hell do you mean you can't do this right now? Becky, YOU'RE PREGNANT!" she screamed at the top of her lungs.

"Mom, please," I mustered out through my sobs.

My mom and I continued to argue back and forth, crying and pleading with each other within our conversation. Just when I thought it couldn't get any worse, my dad and little sister got home from an all-day farm auction. Immediately, my dad asked what was going on and my mom broke the news to him. She did not tell him that Roy had got me pregnant, but led him to believe it was Brice. My mom knew my dad probably would have killed Roy if he had known. How we were going to keep this a secret was beyond me.

My dad immediately stormed out the door to go to the barn. He was pissed, but he didn't say a word. My mom did all the talking. Eva was shocked and wanted to ask a thousand questions. My mom told her to shut up so she could think and sent her outside to the barn with my dad. Right as she said that, our phone rang. We all looked at each other, terrified. After the third ring, my mom got up.

"Hey Dawn, can you come over?" I heard my mom ask her.

"No, it's not okay, and I need to talk to you, alone if that's possible." I could only hear one side of the conversation.

"I'll explain everything when you get here… okay, bye." My mother hung up the phone.

She looked at me and said, "Dawn is on her way."

My stomach had been churning the entire time my mom was on the phone, but knowing what was about to go down meant I had to run into the bathroom to throw up. Every nerve in my body was firing in full swing. After I washed my face with cold water, I heard a car door slam. I made it back into the living room and took a seat on the couch. Within a minute, Dawn was knocking on our door. My mom let her in.

"You can have a seat, Dawn," my mom said politely.

"No, I'm fine, just wondering what the hell is going on," Dawn seemed a little defensive.

"Becky's pregnant," my mom told Dawn. I could practically hear Dawn's heart pounding out of her chest. I sat there staring at the floor. I really didn't know what to expect, and apparently, neither did Dawn. She stood there and said nothing for a good five minutes. The silence was so awkward.

My mom finally broke the silence, "It's Roy's. Apparently, he's been sleeping with my daughter since she started babysitting."

Dawn was stunned. She just stood in the doorway and didn't say a word. My mom gave her a moment before she continued.

"Dawn, our family does not believe in abortion," my mom spoke softly. Tears started pouring down Dawn's face. She was trying to process everything. I could see her knees buckling a little as she grabbed the door frame.

"I have to go," Dawn said and turned to walk out the door. We heard the car start and speed off up the road. My mom and I sat there for about thirty minutes in complete silence. That was the first time I had heard the word abortion. I knew in my heart I would never want to kill a baby, but I was so scared. I couldn't see how I could care for a baby. I was still in high school—about to be a junior.

My mom finally let it all out, "Becky, I know you're scared. Please understand this is not your fault, but with God as my witness, I cannot let you abort this baby. You are carrying an innocent child that has done nothing wrong. Do you understand what I'm saying?" I nodded my head *yes* and she continued, "I will take care of the baby when you are in school. We will find a way to provide for this child, okay?" I nodded *yes* again. "It's going to be okay," she said, and then the phone rang.

My mom answered the phone. It was Brice. My mom didn't think it was a good idea that I talk to him, but I wanted to hear his voice.

"Hey, Brice," I said, still sniffling from crying so much.

"Hey, baby, what's wrong with you?" He sounded so concerned. I completely broke down sobbing.

"Brice, I'm pregnant," I finally spit it out. There was nothing but silence on the other end.

"Brice, are you there?" I said after a good five minutes had passed.

"Yea," his voice cracked. "Whose baby is it?" he asked.

I paused for just a moment. "Roy's," I broke down again.

"That son-of-a-bitch," Brice was angry. "Hey Becky, let me call you back a little bit later. This is a lot to take in at one time."

"Okay," I did not want to let him off the phone, "I love you."

"I'll talk to you later," Brice said and hung up the phone.

My heart was broken. More than anything I wanted to be with Brice. I experienced the same rejection I felt when the girls wouldn't talk to me. I felt so alone in such a big world. I retreated to my room, where I stayed until the next morning.

It felt weird not having to get up to go babysit. My mind began to wander like I was lost in the woods. I wondered if Brice was ever going to talk to me again. To think that he wouldn't made my heart ache. I wondered what Dawn had done after she left our house. Would she stay with Roy? Was Roy going to show up at my house and kill my family? I wondered how the girls were doing. Did they tell their mom what happened?

Even though everything looked the same in my house, my sense of normalcy literally changed overnight. My future was forever altered at the hands of a predator.

Baby Tina

My mom was up and writing stuff down on a piece of paper the next morning. She had the phone book opened up to the yellow pages.

"What are you doing?" I asked.

"I'm thinking about what we need to do to provide for this baby. You know, like stuff we'll need and the different agencies that will help with your pregnancy." My mom knew the ins and outs of government assistance, as we had been on it my whole life.

"What about the baby?" I asked.

"What do you mean, 'what about the baby?' I thought I was clear yesterday. You'll have this baby, and I will care for him or her while you're in school," she stated.

"What about Roy? What's going to happen with him?"

"Becky, I don't know what's going to happen to Roy. He can burn in Hell as far as I'm concerned. I can't understand what the hell was going through his head. He can't even take care of his own damn family, let alone this baby. He will not have any part in this baby's life. Do you understand that?" My mom seemed agitated when I brought his name up.

At that time, I was okay with that. I didn't want Roy anywhere near the baby I was carrying because I knew he was a monster. I did not disclose the torment that he had put me through because I still held an underlying fear of him. I wasn't sure about what happened between him and Dawn, but I was about to find out.

Right about lunch time the phone rang. It was Brice.

"Hey," I said, unsure of where we stood in our relationship.

"Hey," he replied back sounding like he was trying to hold back.

"What's going on?" I questioned.

"I went to Roy and Dawn's last night. That ole dumb bastard said you were hot after him. That he couldn't even be around you without you trying to get in his pants. He told me he finally gave into you, and he thinks you set him up because you thought he'd leave Dawn," I could hear Brice's heartache through the phone.

"Brice, that's not true. I never ever wanted Roy. I was scared of him," I pleaded back with him.

"Well, that's not what Roy is saying. It's just a lot of information to take in right now," Brice said.

"How do you think I feel?" I came back quickly.

"I guess you're pretty scared. Are you keeping this baby?"

"I have no choice, Brice. I'm not having an abortion," I said firmly.

"Roy thinks it's my kid…" he stopped talking.

"Brice, you and I both know this is not your baby. Roy was the only person I had ever been with, and it wasn't by choice," I stated matter-of-factly.

"Well, I don't know what the hell is going on. Roy's got everyone confused saying it's my kid and you came on to him. He's pissed. Dawn's pissed. I'm pissed."

"At who?" I immediately demanded. "Brice, this is not my fault. I did not do anything wrong. You have to believe me," I started crying.

"I don't know, Becky. It's just a lot. I just need some time. I really like you, but I don't think I can do this. I don't know if I want to get involved in all this. I'm really sorry," Brice was breaking up with me. My life was over. The only guy I ever loved was dumping me because of Roy. I cried and cried, and then cried some more. Why was Roy doing this to me?

It wasn't until the following week that Dawn reached out to my mother. She stated that she and Roy were staying together, and they wanted nothing to do with the baby I was carrying. She wanted to know our intentions, although she also stated that Brice had relayed that I was keeping the baby. Dawn wanted to ensure that neither the baby nor I would ever contact Roy again. She obviously believed the bullshit story Roy fed her. I wanted nothing to do with Roy, but my heart ached because she held such a hatred in her heart towards me.

Even at that time, I still had not revealed the complete truth about Roy raping me to my mother. I don't know why I didn't tell, although I know fear was a factor. My dad was still under the assumption that it was Brice's baby. He thought Dawn was handling the matter on Brice's behalf. He also assumed because I was pregnant, Brice jumped ship; he wasn't about to be responsible for a baby. I hated that my dad thought like that because deep down, I still loved Brice. Honestly, I think my dad would have killed Roy had he known the truth.

My mom agreed to the terms of Dawn's request. We were both upset about Dawn's reaction, and neither one of us could believe she had sided with him. There was nothing else to do until the baby came. School was about to start the next week, so that became my focus.

School had never been my strong suit, as I had struggled academically my whole life. As my stomach started getting bigger and bigger, I became the outcast I never asked to be. Some kids made fun of me because I was pregnant, some shunned me like I had the plague, and my one true friend's parents told her she was no longer allowed to hang out with me. I would occasionally see Amy in the hallways, but she never talked to me. Actually, she avoided me just like everyone else.

The pregnancy made going to school unbearable for me. The endless ridicule I felt every day was too much for me to handle. The mental toll was almost worse than being raped by Roy. I asked my mom if I could quit school, and, surprisingly, she said yes.

I felt an undeniable freedom when I dropped out of school. No more bullying. No more snotty looks. No more jokes. No more homework. No more shame. I felt freed from so much pressure.

I spent most of my days on the couch in front of the television, not understanding the lasting impact that would have on my life. The bigger I got, the more uncomfortable I became. By this time, I knew I was having a girl. I hadn't shared that with many people because I didn't have any friends. I was happy that I was having a girl so that I could bond with her. In my mind, she would be my best friend.

On April 5th, which was also my due date, I felt severe pain in my stomach. My mom recognized it as labor and drove me to the hospital. By the time we checked in, my labor was so painful that I thought I was going to die right there in the hospital. My mom was a huge help during delivery, as she was able to coax me through labor. She was my voice, as the doctor and nurses seemed very unsympathetic to my situation. My delivery was quick with no complications. My new best friend, Tina, was perfect and the most beautiful baby I had ever seen.

Two days later, we were both released from the hospital. I was excited—and scared—to have my new bundle of joy. I felt comfortable knowing that my mom would be with me twenty-four seven to help me care for her. There was no turning back; it was official—I was a mom.

Life transitioned pretty easily with Tina at home. I had a real live baby doll that I loved more than anything in the world. I lost lots of sleep, but overall, she was a great baby. My mom constantly schooled me on taking care of Tina properly over the next few weeks. I felt like I was doing pretty well as a teenage mom. She was growing and meeting all her baby milestones. I couldn't have been happier.

June had rolled around and the weather was perfect. I asked my mom if she could take us out for some ice cream, to which she said yes. I got Tina strapped into her car seat and hopped in the back with her. Eva jumped in the front with my mom. We made it to the Tasty-Freeze and enjoyed our afternoon treat. As we were leaving, my mom said she needed to stop by the store for some soda. After we pulled in and parked, my mom dug in her purse for some cash and handed it to me.

"Can you go grab some Coke?" she asked me.

I exited the back seat and made my way into the gas station. And, then, there he was, right in front of me. My heart sank and my knees wobbled. The knots in my stomach made me feel like I was going to throw up.

"Hey Becky, how's it going?" Roy said to me with the same old shit-eating grin on his face, grabbing a twelve pack of beer out of the cooler.

Fear struck me like the plague. "It's fine," I wondered if he could sense my panic. I just wanted to get the soda and check out.

"I'd like to spend some time with you and the baby if I could. She's about three months old now, right?" he questioned.

Was he serious? I couldn't grasp what he was asking. "Yea, she's three months and one week. And I'll have to ask my mom if that's okay if you can see her," I replied.

"Well, I don't think she'd like that too much. Maybe we could meet on the Spivey Road in about an hour? You could say you were going for a walk or something, and I'll come and meet you," he recommended.

"Ah, I guess I could do that," flew out of my mouth. I wanted him to be able to see her. Maybe she would soften his heart and make him want to be a part of her life.

"Ok, I'll meet you shortly," he said.

"Okay," I agreed, completely terrified on the inside. Why I agreed to meet him has haunted me to this day. I left the store before he did, so my mom didn't see him. We arrived at home and I packed Tina up in her stroller. I told my mom I was going out for a walk. I walked a good forty-five minutes up and down Spivey Road before Roy showed up. When he pulled up, he told me to meet him at Purdy Pit, which was a well-known sand pit where kids partied on the weekends. Although I had never been there, I knew what he was talking about.

I pushed the stroller down the tree lined path to where he had parked his van. He got out and oood and ahhed over Tina for about two seconds. He then turned his attention toward me. Within seconds, he had grabbed me and stuck his tongue down my throat. I tried pushing him away, but he had a tight grip on me.

Roy started saying how much he missed me and how he thought about me all the time. He claimed that he was going to try to find a way to give me money to help out with Tina. The entire time he was talking, his hands were all over my body. I told him to stop repeatedly, but he did not.

Within five minutes of seeing him, he had pushed my pants down, tripped me backward onto the ground and got on top of me. He had done it again.

After he raped me, he got up and brushed the sand off of himself. I laid on the ground, stunned. He nudged me with his boot and asked me if I was going to get up. My butt was covered with sand, so I brushed it off as quickly as I could so that I could pull my pants up.

"It was great seeing you," Roy stepped in close to kiss me. He said he had to go and got in his van to leave.

As he drove away, I stood there stunned. Tina was asleep in her stroller. As I looked at her, panic set in immediately. Right then, I was overcome with fear that Roy impregnated me—again. I hadn't had a period since the baby had been born, but that did not matter to me in that moment. All I knew was I did not want another baby.

I pushed the stroller down the path and headed home. I had to get it together. There was no way I could tell my mom what had just happened. She would have killed me. I could only pray like a maniac that I did not get pregnant.

I made it home about forty-five minutes later. Immediately, my mom asked me how my walk went. My heart was pounding out of my chest as I told her it was fine. She then suggested that I continue to exercise to help get my weight down, plus the fresh air would be good for the baby. I agreed with her, but in my mind, was saying 'hell, no, I won't be doing that again.'

I went into the bathroom to clean up as best as I could. I acted as normal as I could, even though, I was far from normal. Everything about the evening continued like it normally would, yet I felt psychotic in my head. I ate dinner with my family, I fed and bathed the baby and I watched television. Nothing was out of the ordinary with my actions.

Then the phone rang. Every negative scenario that I could think of ran through my head within fifteen seconds. I was sure that it was Dawn, or Roy, who would tell my parents everything that happened just hours ago. Imagine my surprise when my mom announced that Brice was on the phone. Nice butterflies filled my tummy, not at all like the knots that happened when I saw Roy.

"Hello," I said with more of a question than a greeting.

"Hey, how's it going?" he asked.

"I'm good, how about you?"

"I'm good too. How's the baby? How do you like being a mom?" Brice said.

"It's not bad. My baby is really good," I couldn't help myself, "What made you call?" I wanted to know, no, I needed to know.

"Oh, I just talked to Roy. He thought I should give you a call," Brice stated. My heart felt like it exploded in my chest. This couldn't be happening. As much as I wanted to stay on the phone, I knew I wasn't going to be able to keep it together.

"Oh. Hey, Brice, can I call you back? The baby is crying," that was the fastest I had ever thought on my feet.

"Sure, I'll talk to you later," he replied.

I hung up the phone with him and raced to my bedroom. I stuck my face in my pillow and let it all go. I could not believe Brice called me at Roy's persistence. My heart ached as though someone put a knife through it.

I called Brice back the next day, but his mother said he wasn't home. I asked if she'd let him know that I called. She said she would, but I never heard back from him.

A few agonizing weeks went by, but I finally started my period. I was still a little nervous at the possibility of being pregnant because I did have one light period when I was pregnant with Tina. Although this period seemed normal for me, deep down inside, I had doubts. It wasn't until I had my fourth and fifth menstrual cycle with no pregnancy symptoms or big belly that I thought I was okay.

Just when I thought I was free and clear, and completely unexpected, Roy pulled up into my driveway. *'Oh my God!'* my insides were screaming.

For a few seconds, I stood there stunned that he had the colossal nerve to come to my house. I had just made it outside and was letting Tina, who was about nine months old, play in her sandbox. She wasn't walking yet, but she could crawl. Roy pulled up close to the sandbox.

Fear paralyzed my insides; I thought my heart had stopped beating.

"Hey, how's it going?" Roy said after he rolled down the window.

"Is anyone home with you?" he asked quickly.

"No, my parents went grocery shopping," I finally spoke.

"I wanted to swing by to give you some money," he claimed.

"Really," I replied. I was shocked with his statement.

"Yea," he stated, as he opened the door to his van and stepped out. He pulled his wallet out of his back pocket and moved around to the side door of his van and opened it.

"Do you want some donuts or pies?" He asked. There were several pallets of baked goods and breads. The smell was heavenly.

"No, I'm fine," I replied.

"Just come look," he ordered. I got up and walked towards the van. Tina watched me as I made my way to the door to peek in at the goodies. Roy held up a twenty-dollar bill.

"Here," he said.

As I went to take the money from his hand, he lunged into my whole body. His hands were all over me, including on my zipper. I could feel a sharp piece of the van door scratch my shoulder.

"Ouch, Roy, stop. Please stop," I pleaded.

"But I've missed you. I want you," he said as he smothered his mouth onto mine. His van was close enough to the sandbox that he was able to stand on the wood that formed the perimeter. He forcefully but quietly moved me over one step.

"Roy, stop. Please don't do this," I begged. He let his hand off my pants long enough to unzip his. He pushed my shorts and underwear down until they hit the ground.

"Please, Roy, don't do this. Please, I don't want to get pregnant. Please don't do this in front of Tina," I cried.

Roy shushed me and stuck his penis inside me. He took three strokes and pulled out. I could feel his semen pour onto the inside of my leg. He quickly put his penis away and zipped his pants. He bent over and grabbed my shorts and underwear and pulled them up for me. I zipped and buttoned them.

"See, Tina didn't even see what happened," he remarked. "I gotta go, but it was great seeing you. I'll swing by and see you again sometime." He kissed me on the lips and grabbed the van door to shut it.

"You want something before I go?" he asked one more time. I said no and stepped out of the way.

"I'll see you later. Buy something cute for the baby, okay?" He walked to the driver's side door and got in his van. He started it up and put it reverse. Roy waved one last time before he put it in drive and left.

I couldn't believe that he just raped me—at my own house. Shock rocked my world. I grabbed a wet one and wiped the inside of my leg. I had taken three more wet ones and wiped myself inside my underwear. Tears streamed down my face as

I watched Tina try to eat all her toys. I loved my little girl, but I hated the way her father treated me. He had so much control over me. I just wanted to move so I would never have to see him again, but I was stuck. I didn't have money or a job, nor did I know the steps to take to make that happen. My life sucked.

I started sobbing uncontrollably while all these thoughts ran through my head. Immediately, Tina started crying too. I picked her up and grabbed her stuff to take her in the house. My stress level was off the chart. Even though Roy felt like he had a fool-proof plan to not get me pregnant, I didn't know if it would work. I was a mess and had no outlet.

I took Tina into my bedroom and we laid in my bed until she fell asleep. My thoughts ran rampant. I kept rehearsing in my head what I could have done differently. Could I have snatched Tina up and ran somewhere? Would he have killed both of us? Or would he have left? Could I have inflicted some kind of pain on him that would send him running? I envisioned grabbing his penis and ripping it from his body. His retaliation to that was severe in my vision, as I saw him beat me to death and then strangle Tina. I figured he would put our bodies in his van and dump us somewhere no one would ever find us.

In my mind's eye, I then thought about Dawn catching him in the act of raping me at my house. Honestly, he had no business being there. I figured she would beat him up for me and then divorce his sorry ass.

All these thoughts completely consumed me. My body was clenched in anger and frustration. I was completely enraged at his boldness and audacity to rape me in my own yard.

Finally, a couple hours later, I heard my parents and sister come home from shopping. My mom immediately asked me if

I was okay. I told her I was and strapped Tina in her high chair so I could carry groceries into the house. I felt like dying, but life continued on like normal, even though *I* was so far from normal.

During my enraged thinking session, I vowed to not have sex with anyone until I got married, including with Roy. I didn't know how I would stop him if I should ever see him again, but I knew that I wasn't going to put myself in any position where I was alone with him.

For the next year or so, I did not see Roy. I occasionally saw Dawn or the girls, but not him. The disgust emanating from them never changed; they hated my guts. I was actually surprised the girls responded that way towards me; after all, they knew what their father had done. I could only speculate that it was their mother's love that made them despise me.

Free to Fly

It was my eighteenth birthday. My parents took me, my sister and Tina out to dinner to a popular restaurant in the next town over. The young man, Mark, that waited on us was so friendly—almost overly friendly. By the time we were ready to leave, my mom gave him our phone number. During our dinner, he found out that the two-year-old was mine, and that I was single. I guess that was enough for him because he called me the next day and asked me out on a date.

I was happy to be going out again. It had been years since I had been out. Brice was the only boy I dated, and I had sex with him once. Of course, Roy was the only man that had raped me, and that happened multiple times. I think being a young mother helped me grow up and mature more quickly, but I wasn't really sure because I lived a very sheltered life. A trip to the grocery store was about the only time I got out of the house. Occasionally, we'd drive to the lake for a picnic, but that didn't happen often. I was a homebody who focused all my time on caring for Tina.

Mark was going to be a brand new experience for me. I wasn't necessarily attracted to him, but I couldn't deny his likability. He was very soft spoken and really sweet from what I had seen at the restaurant and during his call to ask me out.

Mark picked me up the next evening. He was more of a planner than Brice was—he had already told me that we were going out to eat at the restaurant where he worked and then we would go see a movie. I was happy just to be going out.

I figured out from our conversation at dinner that Mark was legit; he wasn't trying to be deceptive in who he was or what he was into. Mark read like an open book. I could ask him anything, and he delivered whatever answer he knew to the best of his ability.

Mark was tall and skinny, with light brown hair and brown eyes. I could tell by his skin tone that he probably struggled with acne as a teenager. Mark was twenty, worked as a waiter, loved going to church and attended college, where he was majoring in business. Mark wanted to work in a corporate setting. I liked that he had goals and dreams, but I felt very beneath him and his big goals.

He wasn't put off that I didn't graduate high school, but he voiced that I could still get my GED. The thought of having to study for the test overwhelmed me. I'm sure Mark could feel my unease, and he offered to help me study. I liked that he wanted to push me out of my comfort zone; I just wasn't sure if I was ready to leave it.

After dinner and the movies, Mark brought me home and asked to see me again. His schedule was tight, but he was going to make sure he at least could swing by the house a couple times a week. I loved the fact that he was so accepting of Tina. He was not scared to hold her or show her affection. Tina was little, but she seemed to like Mark.

Over the next few months, Mark grew on me. He definitely didn't give me butterflies like Brice, but his personality and drive for a better life was attractive. Our bond as best friends was secure. I felt like I could trust Mark and decided to share the truth about Roy with him.

I confessed every single gory detail that Roy put me through. Mark listened intently, asking few questions so I could say everything I needed to say. He was so non-judgmental—something I definitely needed to confirm my sanity. I think my confession drew us closer together. That night was the first time I felt really connected to Mark. It finally felt like I loved him.

Mark said very little as he absorbed my story. He wasn't overreacting and he was very apologetic that I had endured such trauma at such a young age. He vowed to always be Tina's and my protector, no matter what happened between us. Everything about our relationship-slash-friendship was moving in the right direction. Mark was very structured and disciplined, something I was learning to be along the way by being with him.

Within a few months of hanging out with Mark, he kept his word and helped me study to get my diploma. I received my GED and got a job at the daycare center in town. It was my first job ever, and I loved that Tina could go to work with me. I did have to rely on my mom to get me back and forth to work, but Mark assured me that studying for my driver's license would be next.

One thing I could say about Mark was he kept his word. Not only did he teach me how to drive and obey the road signs, he read the driver's education book with me. A few weeks later, I was no longer at my mom's mercy, as I could take her car to work when she didn't have anything to do that day.

Another side of Mark that I deeply admired was his devotion to God. I started to attend church, where he had been a member his whole life, with Mark. Despite the church members knowing that Mark was not Tina's biological child, I never felt judged and they accepted us with open arms. It was really nice to be loved by complete strangers. Church was a peaceful place, filled with a lot of affection. It was definitely something I wasn't used to.

Around my tenth visit to the church, I had an experience that would forever change my life. The pastor was doing a sermon on letting go of our past hurts and pains. I was all ears, of course, especially with what had happened with Roy.

As he shared his story about an uncle that had sexually abused him, I could feel myself tensing up, reliving the repeated rapes. It was like everything was coming back to haunt me right there in the church. The pastor, right in the middle of service, asked those who had been abused in some way to step forward. He wanted to pray a special prayer over them.

Mark nudged my side, and I gave him an 'I'm paralyzed with fear' look. Mark then pushed my elbow a little and I stood up. "You can do this. God is with you," he said. I was a brand new believer, not quite sure about anything.

I stepped into the aisle and walked toward the altar with tears streaming down my face. I was trembling with fear, uncertain of what was about to happen. I was comfortable at Mark's church, but I was comfortable in my seat, where I wasn't the center of attention. Now all eyes were on me while I walked what felt like a million miles to the front. I couldn't even tell you if anyone else made it to the altar; my walk was so surreal. Every emotion imaginable went through me with each step I took, but I made it.

As soon as I stepped onto the altar, the pastor took three steps forward to meet me. Although I was taller than him, he stared into my eyes and said, "Young lady, God loves you." As he was talking, his hand was stretched forth as if he was going to touch me. I am unsure if he actually put his hands on me because I hit the floor. I was conscious of where I was, and I could hear the congregation gathering around me, but my attention was on the movie-like scene playing out in my mind's eye and on the tingling sensation running through me.

As I was laid out on the floor, I felt a surge of power run through my body. It was like sticking a knife in a light socket, minus the pain. It started at the top of my head and when it got to the bottom of my feet, I felt it leave my body. I saw a dark cloud-like ball of fog and was thinking that was a weird thing to see in church, and did that come out of me? And then the tingling sensation started again from the top of my head to the bottom of my feet. There was another ball of fog, although this time it was lighter in color. Then a third time, it happened again, except this time it was like a white cloud. A manly figure was standing in the cloud and he spoke to me. "You believe, my child," was all he said. It was so peaceful.

As I continued to lay on the floor, everything in me and around me felt so incredible, like the weight of the world had been lifted off my shoulders. I felt so loved, unlike anything I had ever experienced before. I felt so free, like I could move forward in my life joyfully. I felt so forgiven, like my past could no longer haunt or torment me.

As I opened my eyes, there were several members holding hands in a circle around me. Mark was standing on the side of me and I immediately locked eyes with him. His smile spoke volumes. I could see tears welling up in his eyes, but he didn't have to say a word. I knew something miraculous had just happened, but I was still trying to catch my bearings.

Finally, one of the church members asked me if I was okay. I replied with a *yes*. Although it was me speaking, I sounded different. Heck, I felt different. A couple of the ladies extended their hands to help me up. As I stood up, I felt like I could breathe better. I felt lighter like I instantly lost one hundred pounds. I exchanged a few hugs with a couple of the ladies and then made my way back to my seat.

The pastor said a few words, but I was in such a happy, restful place that I did not hear any of it. Church let out early that day, and I continued to bask in the glory that was within me. I wasn't sure if I should share my story with Mark or not. My experience was so real and so pure that I wanted to, but I didn't want him to think I was a nut job.

Over the next few months, I attended church as much as I possibly could. Some of the women volunteered to help me study and understand the Bible. They were interested in me and in my growth. I felt so loved by these newfound friends. Mark was truly excited about my interest in church and the Word.

My tragic past seemed so distant, almost like I could have an out-of-body experience while sharing my past with just a couple of the women. Although they assured me that it was not my fault, they were also sympathetic with my choice to not want to report it to the police. I didn't want to ruin any more lives, even though the family hated me.

God had set me free from all the damage Roy had bestowed upon me. I felt alive for the first time ever, like I had a purpose and power to live. I no longer felt guilty or suffocated over the tragic and heinous acts that Roy seared into my long term memory. God was my saving grace. Nothing could separate me from the Lord's love, and Mark watched me transform before his very eyes. He truly loved the woman I was and continued to become.

Mark and I dated almost two years before we got married. Because Mark was such a gentleman, I kept my word and did not have sex with him until our wedding night. God supplied me with the perfect man. I knew my life would be stable and secure forever because I believed and counted on my Lord and Savior, Jesus Christ. Nothing and no one could take that away from me.

Our wedding was low-key but beautiful, with only our small church family and a few relatives in attendance. I didn't need anything extravagant, as I was more than ready to be Mark's wife. I was, and still am, forever grateful for Mark. I may have never had the opportunity to understand how much God loves me if I hadn't met him in the restaurant where he worked that one fateful night. I guess God had the best birthday gift for me that night.

Even more than God's love, I understood that I was forgiven and that His Son died for me, and gave me eternal life. My faith and trust was, and still is, in Him alone. My life could have been long suffering instead of long satisfying. My Rock, Jesus Christ, made all the difference in the world.

Immediately after the wedding, Tina and I moved into Mark's house. There is no doubt in my mind that Mark was meant specifically for us. About four months after we were married, I found out that we were pregnant with twins. I was flabbergasted over the news, but I felt like it was doable. Mark was ecstatic. Tina was thrilled, as well. She was about to be a big sister to two brothers.

Life moved forward peacefully. We continued to attend church and took on different responsibilities within the ministry. Mark finally made it into a corporate job at one of the largest banks in the local area. It paid so well that I was able to leave the daycare and stay at home with our children. By this time, Tina was in elementary school and doing well.

Unfortunately, Tina attended the same school as Roy and Dawn's girls. I saw Dawn on occasion, and the look of disgust on her face every time she saw me made me feel sorry for her. I knew that I was not the one at fault for what had happened, and I had been set free from the guilt and condemnation I suffered because of it.

However, I had a hard time grasping why she blamed me for something her husband did. It made no sense, but, and this is a big but, I prayed for her often. I wanted more than anything for Dawn to know God. I knew from experience that He would provide the rest and peace that had to be needed to deal with her husband. I held no ill will towards anyone in that family. In fact, I prayed for them more often than not.

Even though I was completely comfortable with who I had become through Christ, I talked to Mark about the possibility of moving to a neighboring town. Although that would have been ideal, our children would have suffered in a less than desirable school district. Mark had enough logic to know that was not the right option. Plus, he reminded me, we could ultimately set the example for others to follow. Mark stated that there was no need to ever run from our problems with the God we served. We were secure in Him and put on Earth to believe in the one true God.

Mark was wise beyond his young years. He always knew what to say and how to say it to make an impact. I admired him for that.

The Later Years

It had been years since I had seen Roy. I was used to the snobby looks from Dawn and the girls, but Mark and Jesus Christ helped me tremendously to overcome the rejection and hatred they held for me in their hearts. Prayer was my answer. I couldn't control how other people felt or acted, but I could control myself and my reactions. God's grace sustained me through these uncomfortable situations.

Tina was getting ready to turn ten, and I was planning to have a birthday party for her. I had all the cake, decorations and games to be played organized. All we needed was for her guests to arrive.

As I passed by the window, I noticed a truck sitting in our driveway. I continued to gather the plates and forks, believing a child would be knocking on the door any moment. No knock came.

A few minutes later, I looked again. My knees wobbled and I began to shake. Roy was sitting in my driveway. Every fear and emotion from the past ten years rushed over me. Mark was at the store picking up some last-minute items and would be dropping the boys off at my mom's house. Tina and I were at home alone.

My mind raced, trying to figure out my next move. 'God, you're with me. I need your wisdom right now,' I said under my breath.

I was scared to let Tina outside by herself because I had no idea if he would steal her, use her to get to me or even rape her. I had no clue as to his intentions, but I was sure that it wasn't a visit without a reason. Roy had proved on two occasions that he came with a premeditated objective. I definitely didn't want to see him, but I knew he saw me because I had passed by the window. Oh, how I wished Mark was home!

Roy continued to sit in the driveway for about another five minutes. Tina had come out of her bedroom and announced she thought one of her friends had arrived. I did not want her birthday ruined or for her to think of her 'real' dad at this point of her life. I had to do something.

"I think that might be the pest control man," I told her. "Your dad," meaning Mark, of course, "said he saw some mouse droppings and told me to call someone to take care of that. Plus, I don't see any of your friends in that truck. I'll go out there to check," my heart was pounding so hard my ears throbbed. She walked into the kitchen to admire all her decorations as I walked out the front door.

I marched up to Roy's truck beyond scared. "What are you doing here, Roy?"

"Hey, Becky, you look good," he said, with that same old shit eating grin on his face.

"What are you doing here, Roy?" I repeated myself. I purposely kept my back to the house just in case Tina did look out the door or window.

"I came to bring Tina a gift for her birthday," Roy said, with a small bag sitting on the seat next to him. "Is Mark at home?"

"No, Mark's not at home," I said, looking him square in the face.

"Can I come in for a minute?" Roy asked, still smirking. I could instantly feel that he hadn't changed a bit.

"Sure, you can come in my house and meet your daughter for the first time. All I need to know is if your number is still the same so I can call Dawn to let her know? I'm not about to start any mess, and if she's okay with it, I'm okay with it." I was firm with my words and, I swear, Roy shit his pants right there on the spot. I had never felt more empowered in all my life. Praise the Lord for quick wit.

He stumbled over his words to say that Dawn didn't know he was coming and then asked if I could just keep it a secret.

"Oh, my days of keeping secrets are over. Anyone who wants to know the truth just needs to ask because I will tell it," I was on a roll. "You better let Dawn know you came over because if you don't, I will," I was staring him down as I said this.

"I'm just going to leave. It looks like I'm not wanted here," he said like a fighter who just got his butt beat.

He started his truck and put it in reverse. I turned to walk back in the house and heard the engine right behind me. I stopped quickly and turned around, looking at the truck an inch away from hitting me. I looked at Roy and he had that same smug smirk on his face. "What? My truck rolled forward," he arrogantly stated.

"I'm calling the cops, Roy. You're going to jail." I had my finger pointed directly at him.

His demeanor changed instantly. "I'm leaving, I'm leaving," I could see the panic in his eyes as he stepped on the gas to back up.

"Don't forget to tell your wife because I'm going to call her, and hey, Roy, don't you ever come to my house again, do you hear me?" I yelled out in the driveway. I saw him nod his head *yes* as he was leaving. He looked terrified like he had just seen a ghost.

I hurried into the house and locked the door behind me. I gave myself just a few seconds to thank God that no hurt, harm or danger happened. I went to the phone and immediately called my mother's house to see if Mark was there. My mom told me he'd just left to go home and that he should be there within the next ten minutes. Fortunately, and to the best of my knowledge, Tina missed the entire incident. Five minutes later, Mark pulled in. Because Tina was excited about her day, I pulled Mark outside to let him know everything that happened. He was so proud of me taking a stand against Roy. Mark wrapped his loving arms around me and told me he loved me.

Considering my history with Roy, Mark thought it would be best to report that he had come over. Mark convinced Tina to run to the corner store with him so I could make the call to the police. The 911 operator didn't seem impressed with my story. I didn't care and asked to be contacted by someone that could record the incident. I also reiterated that it would have to wait until Monday, as I didn't want to have to explain anything to Tina. The operator claimed she would pass the information along.

I felt a little on edge for the rest of the day, even though I was definitely the victor in the situation. Mark continued to reassure me that Roy would never be back, which I felt in my heart, but at the same time, I knew Roy was a ruthless human being. However, I also knew predators hated to be challenged; I had given Roy the business. Roy had a lot to lose; I did not. I definitely was no longer the weak, frightened fifteen-year-old he had preyed upon many years earlier.

Mark suggested that I take it one step further whenever the police did come to take my statement and report the rape. I didn't feel that would be the right step to take. I wanted more than anything to protect Tina from everything that had happened to me. Plus, I didn't know if it was even possible to report a rape from years ago. I explained to Mark that God had set me free from my past, and I didn't feel that rehashing it would make a positive impact on anyone involved. He honored my wishes to not proceed with reporting the rape and let me make that decision.

With hindsight being twenty-twenty, I wish I would have put this monster away for life. I probably could have saved several women from being tortured by Roy. In my heart, I know that because he came back to me years later, his wickedness had never stopped, and obviously, he'd never been caught or reported. May God's love and healing be on all his victims.

The birthday party was spectacular—for Tina. There were lots of girls squealing, screaming and running through my house. Tina had wished every day was her birthday; I was happy that it only happened once a year. By Sunday evening, all her guests had left and I had my house back in order. I couldn't wait for her to go to school in the morning.

By Monday afternoon, a detective from the nearby precinct had called me. I gave him all the information about Roy coming by my house and letting his truck roll up right behind me. The detective said there was not a lot he could do other than to talk to Roy. I agreed to that, if only to send a message that I wasn't playing.

Since that day, Roy never came back. Of course, I have seen him in passing, but he has avoided me like the plague. My message was clear. I think Dawn even lightened up a little with her looks towards me.

Either way, there is no doubt that I was the winner of this situation. He may have stolen my teenage years, but he can't steal the joy that the Lord has given me. Thank you, Jesus Christ!

In the End

I thank God for his unconditional love and that I will live forever (spiritually, that is). I thank God for the grace He gives me daily, as I have been truly blessed throughout my many years of living.

Throughout the years, did I have some moments of sadness because of him? Sure. After all, I'm still human, but, and this is a big but, I never gave him too much of my time. He was not someone I chose to waste my time thinking about, nor was he someone that deserved to be thought about. I had my thoughts, and I moved forward.

Jesus Christ has given me more than I could ever imagine. I'm so thankful for where I have ended up. I am secure in His gift of eternal life that He freely gives to all of those that believe.

Thank you, Heavenly Father. May He bless the readers of my story!

Author's Page

      Any reader would probably be curious as to how such a story of *The Babysitter, The Lost Innocence of a Young Girl* came to fruition. The answer: I am one of the rapist's daughters.

My sister, Tara, ran into our former babysitter over thirty years later at a local grocery store and confronted her about the day she assaulted her. I referenced this in my story when Tara caught Becky with our half-naked father. Becky explained the situation, just as I have in this story. Becky went on to provide a long, detailed message with the truth of what happened so many years ago.

Although my sister did not ask for an extremely detailed encounter of what took place many years ago, Becky freely gave it. The letter was so explicit that I covered my mouth in utter disbelief as I read it. The brutality of what she confessed was so shocking that had I not lived (and remembered) some of it, I probably wouldn't have believed it.

The things she described my dad doing to her were outrageous, but I knew the man she talked about all too well. I wholeheartedly believed everything she wrote. Her story answered many unanswered questions that I had while growing up.

I knew Becky had gotten pregnant when we were young. Several fabricated stories were made to keep the heat and attention off of what my dad did to her. She was put on blast as the 'bad guy.' We were made to believe that she pursued my dad and that he was a poor man being seduced by a teenager.

That was ludicrous. I remembered her telling him no on more than one occasion. But, see, as children, we were influenced, right or wrong, by our parents.

We were then made to believe that she didn't know whose baby it was because she was the town whore. Then there was always the possibility that it was Brice's. If all that wasn't bad enough, it was silently suggested that we should hate her and the baby she brought into the world.

After Becky got pregnant, the story shifted so that it also became a gold digger situation; she wanted money—what? What a complete joke! We were so poor and there was no way my stingy, psycho dad was going to sacrifice beer and cigarette money to give her any child support.

There was an underlying anger about the pregnancy that could not be justified. My dad made a huge mistake and then had the colossal nerve to pin his bad behavior on his wife and children indefinitely. He had no remorse for the damage he produced. He was sorry he got caught, but that was about it.

Honestly, as I got older, probably in my mid-twenties, I stopped blaming Becky for what happened years earlier. She wasn't the one that took a vow to my mom! What we all seemed to neglect growing up was that my dad was supposed to be loyal. He proved over and over again that he wasn't, nor did he want to be. We lived a childhood that no child should ever have to be exposed to; maybe that will be the next book?

Living with my dad was like living a daily nightmare – I could only wish for Tina's upbringing. In my eyes, she escaped unscathed. She had some normalcy in her life. I thank God for Mark stepping in and providing for her.

At our house, it was always all about my dad. He was a selfish, narcissistic man that was possessed by a demon.

He was such a horrible father that I did not shed a tear for him at his funeral. I know that sounds cruel and insensitive, but I wasn't his only child that didn't cry. I have four sisters that will tell you the same exact thing! None of us mourned his passing. We all cried because my mom cried—her tears brought our tears.

My dad died of cancer—go figure. He smoked like a chimney for almost fifty years. I felt bad for my mom because he left her nothing but heartache and financial distress. He was going to spend all he had and then some, not giving a rat's ass about the aftermath for her—but that's who he was and who he had been all those years.

Into my young adulthood, I found myself, at times, very angry at my mom for keeping us five girls in such a traumatizing situation. I often thought, 'what kind of mother could keep innocent kids in such a demoralizing situation?'

Why she let us suffer unnecessarily at the hands of this sadistic man blows my mind. A part of me knows it was her low self-esteem and self-worth. Another part of me knows she was scared shitless at the thought of leaving. Where was she going to go with five small children? Would he have hunted her down to kill her... probably! She was preyed upon for a reason.

As we got older, my mom did appear to get stronger. She got a voice, even though she was still his servant and slave. By then, I think it was easier for her to stay than to leave. That was fine with me if that's what she wanted to do. I knew that I didn't desire that kind of lifestyle for me or my family.

Like Becky, I found God. What a joy! During the early years of my salvation, I reached out to my dad to let him know that I forgave him for all that he had done to our family. My heartfelt letter had him shedding a tear or two, or so I was told. My intention was not for him to cry, but for him to know Christ for himself. I will know one day whether he took heed to the simplicity of the gospel because, much like Becky, I too know that I am eternally secure in my salvation.

I understand that not everyone will want to seek salvation for an internal healing. There are other paths to find profound peace and happiness. For me, implementing a meditative practice has been very eye-opening; it truly lets me see the world in a different light. And if that isn't an answer, seeking counsel might be. Counselors/therapist can be so beneficial to your mental health. For that reason, included is the National Sexual Assault Telephone Hotline number. 800.656.HOPE (4673)

___One Last Thing...___

It's a tragic story....with a happy ending.

I'd be very grateful if you'd post a short review on Amazon. Your support really does make a difference, and I read all the reviews personally so I can get your feedback and make this book and all future books even better.

Thanks again for your support and may God's grace be with you!

Made in the USA
Middletown, DE
23 September 2021